Donated to the
Library by

CAROLYN BENGSTON

God's Photo Album

"In my cartoons since 1960 I have seen the world through the eyes of children.
Now, in this inspiring book, I have seen God. Mahalo, Kamalii!" – Bil Keane, cartoonist, creator of *The Family Circus*

"God needed to be locked into this great Photo Album to evoke your love, laughter, tears, and joy of spirit.
Happy reading." – Mark Victor Hansen, editor, *Chicken Soup for the Soul* series

"This book is full of refreshing reminders that God's spirit is always speaking." – SARK, author/artist, *Succulent Wild Woman*

"This book started with a Dream. . .you will be completely inspired when you read about the dream, the struggle and the victory of a teacher, her students, and an entire community! The power of your Dreams will come alive—Believe and Achieve! – Rudy Ruettiger

"This book is powerful evidence that our heart's desire is also God's desire for us. Answering the invitation to choose to support what we love allows God to move through us into the world. It restores us to wholeness and makes us the miracle workers that we are intended to be. This book opens our eyes and hearts to what is true and holy all around us, and in us."
– Sonia Choquette, Ph.D., author of *Your Heart's Desire*

"Shelly Mecum's concept is nothing less than a message from God—that we each see God in our own honest, unique way."
– Suzanne Falter-Barns, author of *How Much Joy Can You Stand?*

"This book delights the eyes of the heart! When the heart sees, it sings. When the heart sings, it soars.
Open this book. Let your heart see, sing and soar!" – Dale Smith, author of *The Rabbit and the Promise Sign*

"And God said, 'Remember always, the helping hands you're going to need the most in life I have placed at the end of your arms.'"
– Bryce Courtenay, author of *The Power of One*

I dedicate this book:

To the village that met the challenge
and helped us realize a dream for the children and their families.
To my children at home, John and Joey,
and all my children at school.
I love you. You make my heart sing.

To Mother Teresa, Mem Fox and Dr. Hélène Laperrousaz
—my ideal teachers.
To my mother and father, Jeannette and Richard Foco,
who taught me how to walk and then to fly.

To my husband Bill. You are the wind.

GOD'S PHOTO ALBUM

How We Looked for God and Saved Our School

SHELLY MECUM

And the Children and Families
of Our Lady of Perpetual Help School

Foreword by Wally Amos

HarperSanFrancisco
A Division of HarperCollins *Publishers*

A BOOK LABORATORY BOOK

HarperCollins books may be purchased for educational, business, or sales promotional use.
For information please write: Special Markets Department, HarperCollins Publishers, Inc.,
10 East 53rd Street, New York, NY 10022.

HarperCollins Web site: http://www.harpercollins.com

FIRST EDITION
The author is donating 85% of her net royalties to a foundation supporting the school and its projects.

Library of Congress Cataloging-in-Publication Data
Mecum, Shelly.
  God's photo album : how we looked for God and saved our school / Shelly Mecum and
the families and children of Our Lady of Perpetual Help School ; foreword by Wally Amos.
    p. cm.
  ISBN 0-06-065453-8 (cloth : alk. paper) -- ISBN 0-06-065454-6 (paper)
    1. Spiritual life--Catholic Church. 2. Presence of God. 3. Our Lady of Perpetual Help
School (Ewa Beach, Hawaii) I. Our Lady of Perpetual Help School (Ewa Beach,
Hawaii) II. Title.

  BX2350.2 .M413 2001
  282'.9693--dc21

                                                        2001016963

ISBN 0–06–065453–8
ISBN 0–06–065454–6
01 02 03 04 05 QWH 10 9 8 7 6 5 4 3 2 1

CONTENTS

NO GOAL OR DREAM IS TOO BIG!

Sometimes you just have to take the leap

and build your wings on the way down.

Kobi Yamada

D O YOU BELIEVE IN MIRACLES? SHELLY MECUM DOES, BECAUSE SHE WAS THE CATALYST FOR A MIRACLE THAT HAPPENED IN THE MOST UNSUSPECTING PLACE, EWA BEACH, A SMALL COMMUNITY IN THE WESTERN CORNER OF THE ISLAND OF OAHU, HAWAII. *GOD'S PHOTO ALBUM* IS THE RESULT OF THAT MIRACLE.

Shelly was a new reading/literature teacher at Our Lady of Perpetual Help School. This small Catholic school, located in a town where sugarcane once reigned, was in danger of closing its doors due to dwindling enrollment. After a voice whispered to her one evening that a book would be the vehicle to save the school, Shelly began a journey down a road paved with love, prayer, and faith. Brandishing the naiveté of a child and a deaf ear to the word *no*, she mobilized the community to save its school. No one was beyond her reach. She sought and received the support and prayers of everyone from Nelson Mandela to Mother Teresa's order in Calcutta to the *Oprah Winfrey Show*. She wore down hard-nosed business types with her passion, determination, honesty, and sincerity in seeking the resources needed to find God on Oahu.

God's Photo Album, a powerful example of what one person filled with love, faith, passion, and a selfless desire to serve can accomplish, proves once again that individuals, not committees, inspire people. *God's Photo Album* is about more than personal strength; it's about strength in numbers. Think about it. A community comes together to save a school. Children, parents, teachers, businesses—everyone joins forces to achieve a common goal.

I believe there is a Shelly Mecum in each of us waiting to come forth, and I am convinced that reading *God's Photo Album* will help unleash the Shelly Mecum in you. It is hidden in that place within us that knows the answers and solutions always come with the idea. When we listen, as Shelly did, we are encouraged to keep going until we succeed. No goal or dream is too big!

This book is about a strong, living faith supported by love. It's about a really *big* goal and about trusting God to help fill in the pieces. What a great way to start the twenty-first century, reading a book that helps you believe in the power in you. Read on and see what miracles you can create.

Wally Amos

Shelly Mecum, teacher

NO ONE HEARD THE THUNDER

WHERE DID *GOD'S PHOTO ALBUM* BEGIN? AND HOW DID A SMALL ELEMENTARY SCHOOL IN RURAL EWA BEACH, HAWAII, TWENTY-FIVE HUNDRED MILES AWAY FROM MAINLAND U.S.A., TAKE ON SUCH A DARING, ENORMOUS TASK ... AND SUCCEED? IF PRESSED FOR ONE ANSWER, THEN I MUST AFFIRM THAT *GOD'S PHOTO ALBUM* WAS AN ANSWER TO PRAYER, PRAYER VOICED IN SORROW OVER THE POSSIBLE CLOSURE OF A BREATHTAKING SCHOOL ON THE EWA PLAIN. Our Lady of Perpetual Help School, named after a powerful title of Mary, Mother of God, remains standing strong and proud. Heaven helped this little school. Love was the engine. Prayer was the fuel. And God was the driver who steered this school on a journey of faith to places unimaginable and undreamed.

It is not surprising that God should love this school so very much. After all, it is a slice of heaven here. Nine teachers devote their time to each other and the children. The principal waits at the gate each morning to greet children and their parents by name. The staff works tirelessly and cheerfully to meet the needs of the faculty and children. Grandfathers and fathers beam as the children run free on the freshly mowed lawn—their labor of love committed each Saturday morning. Grandmothers sit with and pray for the children in Mass. And the children? The children who share this journey in life grace each step of the path with their daily acts of compassion.

The school grounds are saturated with such a gentle love that young hearts find it difficult to leave at the close of the day. Our Lady of Perpetual Help School is home for many. Auntie Vangie,

Air Survey Hawai'i, Inc.

our school secretary, runs off to a fast-food restaurant to purchase lunch for a child who forgot to bring food from home. Auntie Tessie, our teacher's aide, reaches into her pocket to float children loans for treats at the snack bar. Always a hug can be had, or a tear wiped, or a giggle shared with our Auntie Vangie and Auntie Tessie. Our Grandma Sophie bakes cakes for the children and comes to share her stories. Auntie Lulu and Auntie Julie freely share their love of music with the children. Some children quietly strum the chords of their ukuleles while walking to get a drink from the fountain thanks to our Auntie Pat. Our Auntie Eufemia lovingly cleans the classrooms so our children can learn and play in cheery surroundings. The fire chief and his wife, Allison, build and nurture many fine athletes.

Beauty surrounds the children and softly bathes each school day with dazzling colors. Newly hatched monarch butterflies swirl across the playing field as the children kick balls back and forth or trade cards. A class sits on the grandstand to observe and draw the thickly shadowed Waianae Mountain Range in the distance. The trade winds blow gently through the classrooms, carrying the heady blossom scents from the nearby plumeria trees. Students sit and eat their lunches at brightly painted picnic tables shaded by swaying palm trees. The flowers of the hibiscus are alive with the buzzing of the bees. Graceful egrets—miniature white swanlike creatures—swoop in for cool refreshment from the water sprinklers. The crowing of the rooster next door competes with the echoes of the multiplication-table drills. And songs fill the air throughout the day. On rainy days, the sudden appearance of a rainbow calls classes to pause in wonder. An ethereal goodness permeates each day spent on lessons learned in the classroom, on the playground, and in the church next door.

Ewa Historical Preservation Society

No one saw the storm clouds gathering in the distance. No one heard the thunder. The laughter of the children drowned out the rolling rumblings nearby, harbingers of peril to the future of our school. Lives in Ewa were structured around the sea of sugarcane fields that grew tall here for more than a century. The managers' sprawling plantations were built alongside the workers' simple single-wall homes. All who lived here and worked the land were one big calabash family—brother and sister, auntie and uncle, grandma and grandpa. This is "the gathering place." People from around the world have transplanted themselves here and grown roots that have intertwined with those of their neighbors. So connected are these roots that they are family.

The land itself is flat, barren, and hot. This is the leeward side of the island, so very little rain falls here. Locals call this the desert of Oahu. Even scorpions live here. The only respite from the oppressive heat is the nearby ocean.

Yet life here held a softness once. Back when the land grew sugar, life was sweet in Ewa. Jobs were plentiful. Homes, families, and friendships were nurtured by toiling together in the red sun-baked earth, growing the cane.

When the sugar plantation closed its doors forever, those who lived, loved, and worked here had to suddenly seek jobs in town, far from home, in the land of the vacationers. At dawn they would leave for work. At night they would return home to sleep. Ewa Beach became a bedroom community.

Bankruptcy was rampant. Families found themselves homeless. They resorted to living on the beaches, beneath ramshackle dwellings built from palm fronds. Ewa Beach homes, once so open to one another, were quickly secured behind steel gates and locks, for intrinsic to such desperation and despair are danger and insecurity.

Despite a fierce optimism seen in the whirlwind construction of malls, golf courses, and palatial community developments, fatigue is heavy in the air at Ewa Beach, a fatigue that eventually settles into the spirit.

Ewa Historical Preservation Society

Ewa Historical Preservation Society

The typical parent works three jobs just to pay the monumental mortgages and keep food on the table. An education at a private school is daunting for most. Parents have to make extraordinary sacrifices just to send their children to Our Lady of Perpetual Help School. Those who make this sacrifice sometimes falter midyear, and the child must leave due to financial dilemmas.

This economic reality played havoc on our school's enrollment. The classrooms would shrink, then expand, then shrink again in a matter of months. At first the fourth graders' motto was "Eleven Is Heaven!" That soon changed to "The Twelve Apostles," then sadly was returned to "Eleven Is Heaven!"

Each time a child departed the desk was emptied, the textbooks returned, the lei and farewell hugs sadly given. Tears were shed over the loss of friend and pupil. Prayers were offered for weeks in memory of the missing classmate. Life moved on.

With each child who walked out of the classroom, the risk of closure grew greater. A classroom size of eleven is wonderful for both teacher and student but disastrous for the well-being of the school itself. On one level, as a faculty, we recognized this and were filled with concern.

The rumblings of danger became more apparent in faculty meetings. Time was now spent brainstorming for ways to market the school. A worried principal repeatedly requested the faculty to toot their horn more often. This met with resistance. It flew in the face of a greater principle, that of extolling the virtues of humility. But the school was in mortal danger. This was no time to be humble. The trumpets and trombones and kazoos should have been whisked out, and we all should have played them as loudly and boldly as we could. Instead, however, the faculty and staff continued quietly working, teaching, and loving, in complete denial of the impending disaster.

GOD, ONLY YOU CAN SAVE THIS SCHOOL

I T BEGAN WITH A WHISPER. IT WAS NOT MY VOICE. IT CAME THROUGH ME BUT NEVER FROM ME. I WAS SOAKING IN THE BATH WHILE READING THE CHILDREN'S WRITING. THE CHILDREN TENDERLY RECORDED WHERE THEY HAD FOUND GOD DURING THEIR DAY. THEIR VISION OF GOD WAS GENTLE, SIMPLE YET PROFOUND. GOD WAS FOUND IN THE SHARING OF FOOD, IN PLAYING PEACEFULLY TOGETHER. HE WAS SEEN IN THE WIND, THE FLOWERS, THE TREES, THE BIRDS. SUCH LOVELY IMAGES OF GOD, STRAIGHT FROM THE HEARTS OF CHILDREN.

I set aside the writing, closed my eyes to rest, and a quiet voice whispered in my mind: "It's a book."

The effect of that simple announcement was joy; a joy so deep it was childlike. I ran to the living room and found my husband folding the laundry. Ecstatically, I jumped up and down exclaiming: "Bill! It's a book! It's a book! It's a book! Oh dear God, it's a book!" Bewildered, he replied: "That's great, honey. But you're dripping all over the floor, and I just mopped."

Oh, but the vision swirled in my head. It was so simple. Send the whole school out in search of God during one school day. Ask the children and faculty to go find God and write about it. Imagine! Where would a five-year-old find God? Where would a thirteen-year-old find God? Then compile their work into a book—for publication. "It's a book." I could see it. The idea utterly thrilled me. To ignite the passion in writing, the power in writing, a teacher must provide a real reason to write! How more real can this experience be? Our children will become authors!

When I was calm, I phoned my mom and dad seeking their counsel. They are my touchstones. They have a clarity, a wisdom, that comes from walking the earth longer. Typically they see things I have missed in the passion of the moment. They saw no flaws.

I was anxious for the weekend to pass so I could share this concept with all the teachers. When that moment came, let's just say they didn't exactly cheer. Only our eighth-grade teacher, Laverne Suster, expressed enthusiasm.

Yes! I had one teacher onboard, and the vision began to grow. We'll traverse the island in search of God. We'll board buses with notebooks, pens, pencils, and … cameras! We will go find God, and when we find Him, take His picture and write about it.

I needed to seek permission from our principal. With passion and fervor, I revealed the plan. This was met with raised eyebrows and a lingering silence.

It was my first year teaching at Our Lady of Perpetual Help School. I had been on the job literally less than two months. Further, I was an outsider. My family had recently moved here from Yokosuka, Japan. I had spent the last nine years in Japan teaching English, writing picture books, and acting on a weekly national television show. To the faculty and staff, I was a fruitcake. Trust takes time to build.

Mr. Sasaki finally broke the silence and recommended I seek a grant to fund the project. *A grant? We need a publisher!* I silently thought. I didn't argue. I *couldn't* argue. I could only walk away. The "book idea" was swiftly abandoned in face of the daunting task of grant writing. Yet I remained haunted by this vision.

      Months later some stunning events occurred, a mix of elation and despair. Our children won the state Nene Essay contest. The Nene Award is given to a children's author for the best book of the year, selected by the children of Hawaii. An essay contest is offered to grades four through six. The winning students attend a press conference and read their essays aloud to the honored author. Only one essay is selected from each grade. Our school won two out of the three possible grades!

      This win shifted the universe and shattered paradigms.

      At recess, I raced out to find our principal and again request permission to pursue my book idea.

"Mr. Sasaki, the children can write! We can write this book! And I know how to do this. The first thing is to find a publisher. But you have to trust me. May I seek a publisher?"

This request was met again with silence and then a quiet "Yes. Go get a publisher."

I was ecstatic! All I could do was beam at the children all day. Hope was a glorious bonfire blazing in that moment in time. That's why the despair that soon followed was so overwhelming. Truly, a tidal wave of despair roared in the next afternoon at the weekly faculty meeting, nearly dousing the flame of hope.

After attending a grim meeting with the finance department, Mr. Sasaki sadly walked the faculty down the road to the possible closure of the school. Dwindling enrollment was chipping away at the foundation of the school's financial survival. Our principal expressed his understanding if teachers needed to seek more stable employment opportunities elsewhere.

Silence washed across the room, a heavy stunned silence. Then an argument brewed. On one side those wanting to save the sinking ship. On the other side, those resigned to letting it go quietly, believing a fight was pointless. Every suggestion raised to save the school was quickly shot down.

I turned to the principal and asked: "Mr. Sasaki, what will it take to make our school strong?"

"A preschool. We need a preschool."

"But how will a preschool help us?"

"A preschool feeds new students into the school. But it also serves to finance the operating costs for the entire school. Typically the monthly fees are higher for a child in preschool."

"Great. How much do you think this will cost?"

"More money than we have, Shelly. I had to borrow money just to pay the teachers through the summer."

"Mr. Sasaki, do you believe in our school? If you believe, then all you have to do is go to the presidents of big corporations here on the island and ask them to invest in a sweet elementary school. Tell them about the wonderful people who live here on the Ewa Plain. Explain to them how this community is in dire need of a preschool."

"No, it's impossible. I can't do that."

"It's just money, Mr. Sasaki. If your faith is large enough, you will convince them to make this investment. You must go straight to the top. You must sell them this dream with all your heart. Mr. Sasaki, Our Lady deserves to be saved!"

I had completely forgotten about all the other teachers in the room. I had completely forgotten I was a brand new teacher addressing the principal. The other teachers had been here before and resignation was clearly etched in their faces. The silence swallowed us all. I held my breath, waiting....

"Shelly, it's too late. Don't you understand? We have run out of time. The finance department will not float us another loan. I have been fighting for this school for five years, Shelly! It's too late. There is nothing more we can do."

The meeting broke up without anyone saying another word.

I came home and said nothing to my children or my husband. I sat silently in a chair and wept. My husband made dinner and tucked us all in our beds. He didn't ask any questions. He knew intuitively that there was too much pain to speak.

How could I love a school so deeply? The answer is simple: the children. I love the children.

My first days teaching at our school, the world lost two great humanitarians: Princess Diana, then, five days later, Mother Teresa. I was jolted by both deaths. Princess Diana had died over the weekend, so I was able to put on a brave face for the children. Not so with Mother Teresa. I dearly loved this woman. She was my ideal teacher. My two classroom rules came directly from a quote from Mother: "We should be a center of compassion where we endlessly forgive."

Rule 1: We will be a center of compassion.
Rule 2: We will endlessly forgive.

Gary Woods

All of my students in grades four through eight learned of her goodness during the first week of school. I learned of her death during Mass with all the children in attendance.

While sitting with my fourth graders, our principal offered the following prayer: "Please keep Mother Teresa in your prayers, for she passed away today."

All of the children in grades four through eight turned in my direction with concern. I was fighting back tears and smiling at my fourth graders, who were immediately in front of me. They looked so worried. I whispered to them: "It's all right, children. I'm just surprised. I didn't know Mother was in heaven, that's all. We should be happy for her." I kept secretly wiping away tears. I didn't want to cry in front of them. Doing so might frighten them. I didn't have any tissue paper and felt helpless.

Kiley Kealoha pulled the ribbon from her hair, gently took my hand, and wound the ribbon around my wrist. She looked long into my eyes and whispered: "It's okay, Mrs. Mecum. You can dry your tears with this."

A deep and abiding love was born in that moment. The compassion and gentleness of the children had captured my heart long before this bleak faculty meeting.

That night I prayed: "God, only you can save this school. But do you want our school to be saved? I love this school, God. I want to save it. But I can't do this alone. No one can. God, I'm haunted by this book. Is it the book that will save the school? If it's the book, I need a marketing angle. Why are we writing this book? It is not enough that we all go out in search of you. Why are we writing this book in the first place? It is in your hands. I leave the future of Our Lady of Perpetual Help School in your hands. I accept your will."

Then I fell asleep. For the first time in my life, I let go and let God handle the details. I slept in peace.

In the morning, curious to know God's decision, I asked simply, "God, have you given it much thought?" One word wafted through my mind: "Literacy."

The prayer was answered! The marketing angle revealed! Literacy! We will take this school mobile—for literacy. We will write this book in one school day—for literacy. After all, teachers long to have their children fall in love with reading and writing. What better way than to have them write a book for real—for publication. Our children will become authors overnight!

Further, this will change the whole relationship between the publishing house and our school. The publisher will become our educational partner. We'll ask the publisher to teach our children the whole life cycle of the book, from the idea to the written word to the publishing house, printer, bookstore, and library. This has never been done! And publishers have a vested interest in building future readers. "God! This is *huge!*"

I raced to school to share the stunning news. Again, the teachers did not exactly cheer. However, I was filled with a fierce hope and certainty. I knew heaven was helping us, and that gave me an absolute resolve.

Later that afternoon I contacted Mutual Publishing, a local publisher. I pitched the idea and gleefully held in my joy when Jane Hopkins, the production director, gasped. She promised to schedule a meeting the following week with Bennett Hymer, the publisher.

On Saturday morning I held a planning session at my home. Only one teacher came—Laverne Suster. Again the vision grew to include the families. The "book idea" became a family literacy initiative! The book would be written by the children and their mothers, fathers, brothers, sisters, aunties, uncles, grandmothers, and grandfathers. Therefore we needed the donation of fourteen motor coaches, three hundred cameras plus the developing costs, three hundred notebooks, pens, and pencils. April 23 was selected as the day we would be "seeking God in the gathering place."

The meeting with the publisher went smoothly. Bennett's only concern was the subject matter of the book: God. "Are you sure it's God you want to seek? How about, 'seeking aloha in the gathering place?'"

This appeared to be a pivotal moment in the publisher's ultimate decision. A long silence hung in the air as I gathered my thoughts quickly and prayed I'd find the words to reach this man.

"No, it must be God," I insisted. "I have to be true to this vision. Remember, it is religions that divide us, not God. The beauty of this quest is that it will nourish the total person: mind, body, and spirit. As teachers, we need to nurture and feed these three essential elements of our children.

"What the children and their families write and photograph will come back to nurture and feed the mind, body, and spirit of the reader. I am certain of that. I do not envision this as a religious book, yet it will be deeply spiritual. Imagine five-year-olds up to eighty-year-olds seeking God and finding Him together as a family—writing a book together as a family. It's awesome. Besides all that, how can I cut God out now? This idea came in answer to prayer. I am firm on this!"

The publisher accepted my explanation and questioned how the proceeds from the book would be utilized.

"Part of the money will fund scholarships for our needy students," I explained. "We also intend to build a preschool."

The publisher accepted this proposal and became the school's first educational partner. Our Lady of Perpetual Help School officially had a publisher! I was delirious with joy during the drive home to Ewa Beach.

Later that day an emergency faculty meeting was held to brief the teachers and the principal. This meeting was a far cry from the last time we had all met. No doom and gloom here, not on this day. There was much joy, laughter, awe, and wonder. God had dropped the lines holding us safely next to the pier. Steering our ship away from the harbor, God guided us into uncharted waters.

During the course of this journey in faith, God remained my steadfast friend and partner. I want you to understand that I was able to do the impossible because God made everything possible. He never left me alone for a moment. He opened every door I knocked on. He sent nothing less than angels when assistance was required. The miracle of this story is simply this: It was always more than the power of one.

Knowing this was a pioneering family literacy initiative, we invited the media to be present when we shared the news with the children. Yes! Our school would host a press conference! A simple enough idea. However, I soon learned that communicating with reporters is difficult. You have to get right to the point, summing up your news story in thirty seconds or less, and with a captivating presentation. You must also find reasons to contact them repeatedly to remind them why they should cover this event. I had to learn how to write press releases. I learned quickly.

I also had to overcome the media's obvious lack of interest. Our school was not famous. It was hard for them to believe that a small rural elementary school could accomplish such a brave feat. Our location added to their doubt. Ewa Beach was not Waikiki.

Days were spent contacting the local and national media. Countless faxes were sent. No return calls. The school was one day away from our "press conference" with not one confirmation from any news desk. I knew the faculty would lose faith in me if the media did not come as I had so naively promised. In tears I confided to Auntie Vangie, and we prayed for help.

One hour later an executive from *Nightline* returned my call. He wanted to know if any local affiliates would be covering this. He recommended I contact their affiliate and tell them *Nightline* is interested. Smiling over the phone I asked, "Couldn't you call them? Wouldn't it be better if *Nightline* contacted their local affiliate and asked them to come?"

He laughed and said he would take care of it. "What's their phone number over there?"

Within minutes our school received confirmation that the press would attend our press conference: the ABC and NBC affiliates.

A media consultant recommended that the children wear flower leis during the press conference. "This would sell to snowy Cleveland." Only problem, this advice came at 5:00 p.m. on the eve of the media event. There was much dismay in the faculty meeting when I shared this suggestion. "How on earth could we acquire 168 leis for our children in a matter of hours?" Simple. I prayed. "God, we need 168 leis by tomorrow. Who do we call?"

My first call to Mylene's Floral Wholesale was the only call necessary. A shipment of flower leis had arrived from Thailand and 130 leis had been sitting in too much water. Visually they were flawless, but they could not be sold due to this damage. Mylene, the proprietor, gave them to us and recommended that we shorten them to string thirty-eight more leis. She also donated some extra flowers.

All we needed was manpower, and within minutes that problem was solved. The Filipino Catholic Club was meeting in one of our classrooms. I spoke to the mothers and grandmothers, asking for their help. Rose Oasay and Julie Torres quickly volunteered to stay and string leis with Miss Cabrera, our English teacher, and dear Auntie Vangie. They stayed beyond midnight stringing flower leis for the children.

The next afternoon, as the children were ushered into the church for the press conference, they were greeted by mothers and grandmothers who gently draped flower leis over their heads and tenderly kissed them. Every child received a flower lei and a kiss. This cast a sense of awe upon our young hearts. The children sat quietly in the pews waiting to learn the great secret that had the teachers dashing around the campus so joyfully. When they understood the news, there were cheers, tears, and hugs.

The memory of that charged moment is etched forever in my heart. A promise was made that day to 168 children, ages five to fourteen, and their families. This promise could never be broken, or dreams and young hearts would be dashed forever. I wanted these children to believe they could fly. I vowed to move mountains before I would ever let those tender wings be clipped.

Officially, *God's Photo Album* began the day our intentions were announced so boldly at our very first press conference, held in the church next to the school. I had six weeks to secure three hundred cameras, fourteen buses, a helicopter, boats, a train, a trolley, and a submarine. (The vision had grown to seek God by land, sea, and air.) Six weeks is exactly enough time if you firmly believe heaven is helping. Without heaven's help, it would be impossible.

Now, there was a great deal to do in a very short period of time. I tried to do everything simultaneously, but as I soon learned, things can fall through the cracks that way. Every spare moment between teaching was spent contacting different companies seeking their practical support. The village was enormously generous. Hopaco Office Outlet was quick to donate the three hundred notebooks, pens, and pencils. Makani Kai Helicopters Ltd. gave us the free use of a helicopter to transport four participants. Kaneohe Bay Cruises quickly agreed to take a group out on their glass-bottom boat. When a submarine company fell through due to scheduling difficulties, an executive from Voyager Submarine— from her cell phone—authorized a private submarine to whisk our families away in search of God. Both the Waikiki Trolley and the Hawaiian Railway Society freely offered their transportation support. Captain Gordie Morris offered to take our children out sailing aboard the *Free Spirit,* a trimaran. "This is for children? Well, I'm the keynote speaker that day for a luncheon, but I can take the children out for a sail in the morning. Sure. Why not?"

I was also pursuing cameras through two major film companies. It was a maze. I left countless voice mails with various executives who would call back and refer me to other executives. I would then leave voice mails with these individuals and wait. I hadn't connected yet with the correct department or individual who could authorize the donation of three hundred cameras and developing costs, but I was meeting with such success elsewhere that I was unconcerned.

The buses? I forgot about the buses.

That's not altogether accurate. I knew we needed fourteen buses. Our coach, Mr. de Laura, spent a lovely day helping Laverne and me determine the routes for these as of yet nonexistent buses.

Oahu is divided roughly into four sections: town (Waikiki and Honolulu), *mauka* (mountain), leeward (the desert), and windward. When you leave one section and enter another, it feels like you're in a whole different country. The sights, sounds, smells, and general pace of life vary greatly from one side of the island to the other. Even the climate is distinct. Only a forty-minute drive separates barren desert from tropical rain forest.

As we planned each route for these buses, we kept these visual delights in mind. We wanted to serve our children and families a feast. I offered my favorite places, which were the common tourist hot spots: Diamond Head, the Halona Blowhole, Hanauma Bay, Ala Moana Shopping Center, and Valley of the Temples with the backdrop of the carved Koolau Mountain Range. "Growing up in Colorado, I never saw mountains that looked like that!" I exclaimed. Mr. de Laura and Laverne smiled knowingly, winked at each other, and wrote down my suggestions. Then the two of them, both born and raised in Hawaii, planned the rest of the routes so our children and families would visit both the real Hawaii and the tourist Hawaii.

Laverne and I depended heavily on Mr. de Laura's sense of how long it would take to get from point A to point B. As a federal fire chief and former tour-bus driver, plotting out the destinations for all fourteen buses was a walk in the park for "Mr. D," as the children affectionately call our coach.

Now, back to the buses. In truth, I didn't forget about them. I simply forgot to contact any of the bus companies to ask them to donate the use of their vehicles for the day.

But unusual support came our way when I received a call from Tomie dePaola's assistant, Bob Hechtel. Tomie, a beloved children's author as well as a literacy advocate, champions the efforts of Read Across America. Earlier I had left a voice mail informing him of our book project. His assistant recommended I contact the *Rosie O'Donnell Show* and gave me the number. "Rosie would just love this—168 kids and their families writing a book together … for publication? This is phenomenal, Shelly!"

We called while we still had the nerve. Bob's introduction was like "open sesame" into the *Rosie O'Donnell Show*. An executive listened intently as Araceli Hurley, our second-grade teacher—and a huge fan of Rosie—gushed on and on. She replied warmly: "Oh, Rosie will love this. Fax me some information, and keep us posted on your progress. Yes, we would love to see this book!"

The path into the executive producer's office of the *Oprah Winfrey Show* was far more arduous. It took us three solid weeks to get past the switchboard to speak with the assistant to the executive producer. Janinne Jurin, our first-grade teacher, won the "Oprah Lottery" and made the call. "Get the fax number, Janinne. That's all you have to do," the teachers cheered her on. When she made the call during recess it was a thrilling moment for us all! Her straight-to-the-point demeanor perfectly suited the personality of the executive producer's office, and we got the fax number!

I kept the *Oprah Winfrey Show* up to date with faxes and phone calls. An executive producer in charge of booking authors squealed with delight when I shared this vision: "Imagine! We are going to send 168 children, mothers, fathers, grandmothers, grandfathers out in search of God on one day. Their ages range from five to eighty years old. They will travel by bus, train, trolley, trimaran, glass-bottom boat, submarine, and helicopter. They'll have cameras, notebooks, pens, and pencils. Their mission? Go find God. When you find God, take His picture and write about it. We will then compile their photos and writings into a book titled *God's Photo Album.*

"How wonderful, Shelly. Do you have this in writing? Could you fax this information over to me? Here's my fax number."

Then I got off the phone and squealed!

Spring break was fast approaching. The local publisher contacted professional photographers on our behalf, and they agreed to come and teach our children how to take quality photographs.

The children were so hungry to learn they were on fire! As a class we would go outside and write descriptive passages and come back and share our work. We had formed our own writing group, which met daily. The children even helped edit my faxes to corporations and dignitaries seeking their sponsorship and endorsements. I was very thankful for their help.

One day, while I was away on a field trip with my fourth graders, an executive from the headquarters of one of the major film companies phoned and left a message. The message was simple and to the point: "No, we cannot donate three hundred cameras or the developing costs."

This was a stunning blow to the project, because it left only one other major film corporation. I had been calling them daily and leaving urgent messages.

...THREE HUNDRED ONE-TIME USE
SPEED CAMERAS "FOR SMALL HANDS THAT TEND TO WOBBLE"...

I had heard nothing from the local branch. I was filled with concern. This event was only three weeks away! Purchasing three hundred one-time-use cameras would cost thousands of dollars. And that didn't even factor in the developing cost!

After school I turned to Mary Ellen Miller, our third-grade teacher. Mary Ellen is the peacemaker and great consoler of our school. I heard her singing sweetly in her classroom and went to her in tears. She responded with love, taking my hands in hers and praying: "God, show us the way. Please guide Shelly to that generous heart who will gift us with these cameras."

I came home from school still deeply troubled. After supper, my husband quietly listened then asked, "Have you called Fuji?"

"You aren't listening. I told you that I have left repeated messages with Fuji, and I've had no response."

"You've called Tokyo? I'm talking about the headquarters. You don't have the luxury of time to go through the local branch."

Immediately I recognized the truth in my husband's words. I left mid-conversation and jumped on the Internet. Within moments I had the phone number and a news photograph of Minoru Ohnishi, chairman and CEO of Fuji Film Company. I called out to my husband, "Bill! I found him! Here's his picture. Oh, he looks so kind. I have the phone number."

"Great! Call him." Bill casually quipped.

Fuji Film was our last hope. If Fuji said no, then what were we going to do? Would they really care about a school in Ewa Beach, Hawaii, all the way from Tokyo, Japan?

The answer was yes. They cared immensely. When I called, the switchboard connected me to Dustin Tomonoh, the assistant to the chairman. I wept on the phone as I explained our great need for their assistance. Dustin gently replied: "Do you mean to tell me, the only thing standing in the way of your children realizing their dreams is three hundred cameras and the developing costs?"

I almost dropped the phone. "Yes!" I cried.

"Well, worry no more. We will serve as intermediaries between you and Fuji Hawaii. Fax the information to us and you will be hearing from them in the morning."

So I faxed all the information to Japan. What I learned the next day is that Mr. Ohnishi himself called Mr. Okutsu, president of Fuji Photo Film Hawaii Inc., and asked him to help us. As it turns out, Mr. Ohnishi is fond of these islands and deeply loves children. By 9:00 a.m., Diane Fukeda, marketing manager of Fuji Photo Film Hawaii Inc., called and warmly stated that they wanted to give us their very best—three hundred one-time-use eight-hundred-speed cameras "for small hands that tend to wobble"—as well as most of the developing costs.

I was ecstatic. I floated back to the classroom and shared the news with the children. Some of them cried. This kind of love from so far away is powerful stuff. The children were deeply moved. We cried. We laughed. We jumped up and down and hugged each other—one big group hug. We finally settled down and tried to focus on a spelling test. But we kept beaming at each other as I called out the word and gave the corresponding sentence. "Number 7, *thankful.* I am truly *thankful* for the love and concern extended to us across an ocean. Thankful. Number 8, *forgetful.* We must never be *forgetful* of the generosity of Fuji Film. Forgetful." We were luxuriating in the moment.

The vision grew to host a literacy gala to honor our returning young fledgling authors. If we were going to celebrate, we should invite dignitaries to honor our children. This was fun. Who should we invite? The teachers and I spent priceless time dreaming up the guest list and sending invitations. We invited Sister Nirmala, the Mother General of the Missionaries of Charity, President Nelson Mandela, all the living Presidents of the United States, John Glenn ("What do you mean he can't come? He has plenty of time to prepare for his launch into space"). We were lost in a dreamworld.

Fortunately, Auntie Vangie noted this and remarked, "Enough of this!"

She then pointed out, "Shelly, you don't have any buses. You better get the buses or this school is not going anywhere. You have less than a month. Bus companies need at least a month to schedule. Soon there will be no need for a gala. Get the buses!"

I was jolted awake. That's right! We didn't have buses! I picked up the phone and immediately started calling different bus companies.

After a few calls, I knew we had a serious problem. We needed a company to donate the use of fourteen buses for the day. Some companies did not have fourteen buses available on that day. Some even said they would charge more than their usual rate. I called Roberts Hawaii, the largest local travel company. Helene Shenkus, vice president of marketing, took down the information, the dates, and the numbers, and promised to get back with me.

I went home and did my homework. Through the Internet, I learned that Roberts Hawaii had a thousand luxury motor coaches available, as well as a hundred school buses. They were perfect! This was the company to which to make such a bold request. I could see our children and families traveling around the island on luxury motor coaches, those beautiful buses that typically transport tourists.

But Roberts Hawaii called back with chilling news. Helene Shenkus, who goes by the name of Sam, gently explained that it would be impossible for their company to accommodate our school's request. All school buses were committed to another program. On the spot I changed the request to luxury motor coaches. After all, Roberts Hawaii had a thousand of these. Surely fourteen are available. The conversation grew more and more passionate in the face of resistance.

"Sam, we need you! Don't you realize what we are planning to do here? We are going to write a book together in one day—for publication! One hundred and sixty-eight children and their families will become authors overnight! Five-year-olds will become authors! What were you doing when you were five, Sam? What will these children do next, once they have climbed this high? Sam! Roberts Hawaii is the only way our children will leave the school grounds!"

Compassion entered on Sam's side, and she advised I re-fax an urgent request for Roberts Hawaii's help, underscoring the fact that this project will collapse without. This was no understatement.

In reality, I had just been given a big fat "maybe." I was thrilled. *Maybe* is so much closer than *no*. A week went by. No word from Roberts Hawaii. Spring vacation was fast approaching. Without a commitment from this tour company, our project was dead in the water. Imagine. We had a helicopter, a trolley, a train, a trimaran, a glass-bottom boat, a submarine, an educational partnership with a local publisher, three hundred notebooks, pens, pencils, cameras, and developing costs all donated for this project. Yet without those buses, our school would be going nowhere.

I tried another approach. I attempted to talk to the president of the company. But it is extremely difficult to schedule a meeting of minds when you do not even know the name of one of the participants. The secretary would not disclose his name. I was so desperate that I called Hillary Clinton's chief of staff to request that the first lady call Roberts Hawaii and make an appointment on our behalf. Ludicrous? Absolutely. The lovely part of this is that the receptionist *did* ask if this was possible. She cared. But there is, unfortunately, this small issue of abuse of power, which prevents this sort of networking.

In prayer during a school mass it became clear that a face-to-face meeting was the only solution. The grandmothers and grandfathers, led by Julia Chun, prayed that our school would find those buses. The principal allowed me to leave in the middle of the school day, and he personally stepped in to teach my students.

Before leaving, I ran to every class and asked the teacher if they as a class would pray that we find the words to move the corporate president's heart. I needed courage. Imagine knowing that 168 children are praying for you. It's a powerful feeling. Laverne and I drove down to the corporate office and declared our intention to meet with the president. The receptionist asked if we had an appointment. "No," I replied. "And we cannot leave until we speak with the president." The receptionist smiled pleasantly and sent for Sam Shenkus, the corporate vice president.

Sam graciously spent more than an hour with us. I reiterated our great need for the donation of these fourteen luxury motor coaches. Without Roberts Hawaii's help, all of our efforts would be meaningless. All of it would be for nothing. The conversation went back and forth. Why it was impossible for the company to help. Why it would be disastrous for our children, the families, and our school if they did not help. After much debate, Sam stated firmly: "Shelly, our answer is no. We would like to help you, but we can't."

Then there was silence. Deafening silence. My heart was breaking. What could I say to this? Where were the words to reach her heart?

"Well, you know what my father always says?"

"No, Shelly. What does your father always say?" Sam quipped impatiently.

"You should be very careful with your no's. You are a big company, the largest tour company in the state. But how great could you have become if you had been altogether generous? Sam, I can't go back and tell those children it's over. 'Sorry children, we can't get buses.' Sam, they believe they can fly. We have convinced them of that. You are asking me to go back, clip their wings, and put them in a cage. And they'll still sing, Sam. But it won't be the same song. It will be a different song, a song I never wanted them to learn. Please, Sam!"

A miracle happened. Sam didn't throw us out of her office. She graciously endured this impassioned plea, then stepped out of the conference room. She returned with this deal: "The cost for fourteen motor coaches is nine thousand dollars. Roberts Hawaii will donate the fourteen motor coaches, the drivers, and half of the cost, $4,500, if you can find us a transportation partner with an 'A' rating to share the expense. That's all you have to do."

I exclaimed, "Sam, we are seventeen days away from our deadline!"

"Yes. That's correct. You have seventeen days to find us a partner. But I have faith that you can do this."

I cheered up a bit. She's absolutely right. That's all we had to do. Find a transportation partner willing to invest $4,500 in our project. Sam even provided us with some names to contact. "Stay passionate. Corporations do not part easily with their money," she advised.

I was a bit anxious, but I knew in less than two hours we had secured a firm commitment from one of the largest tourist operations on the island. I could see those beautiful luxury motor coaches pulling into the driveway of our school. We had seventeen days to find a partner for Roberts Hawaii. How difficult could this be? Truth? It was a nightmare.

I immediately began placing calls to the CEOs of the major banks in Hawaii. When it was discovered that I was a teacher seeking money, the call was quickly rerouted through the dismal hallways of corporate foundations. I say "dismal" because each of these foundations have time frames and rules regulating their financial sponsorship. To win the foundation lottery, you must work your way through the proper channels. You must submit proposals, in writing, in a timely fashion. Those deadlines had long passed before this idea was even born. "If you had come to us nine months ago, perhaps we could have considered your proposal. All of our money has been allocated for this fiscal year."

The other obstacle was that the funding had to come from a corporation with an "A" rating. The funding could not come from an individual. The "A" rating meant the company grossed in excess twenty-five million dollars a year. This canceled out any parish bake sales. But I wasn't too worried. Many corporations fit that category. What is $4,500 to a company so very blessed with that kind of annual gross? Apparently, everything. Sam was right. Corporations do not easily part with their money. I needed all of the passion I could muster just to keep the desperate edge out of my voice during each and every phone call. But the days were ticking away, one by one. It was getting more difficult to keep this anxiety hidden during each call.

Spring break arrived, and I could spend every waking moment in pursuit of this transportation partner. I even had a game plan. The morning would be spent contacting corporations on the East Coast. Because of the six-hour time difference, I could begin telephone contact at 3:00 a.m. During the early afternoon I would call West Coast corporations. In the late afternoon I would begin contacting local companies. The evening would be spent researching new companies to contact the next day.

Every morning I would wake up to this sober fact: We were less than two weeks away and still had not found a transportation partner. My confidence was beginning to waver.

I would speak to thirty or more companies a day. I felt hopeful when the executives would ask me to fax them the information. But days later they would call back and gently announce the verdict: "I'm sorry. We wish we could help you, but we simply cannot move that quickly. We have protocols that must be strictly adhered to." Every corporation had their own lovely way of saying no.

Yet every corporate executive unabashedly agreed to my request to please keep us in their prayers. Imagine that! Who did I call? Everyone and anyone. It was a who's who list in the world of business. Every industry was represented. Approximately every five minutes I placed a long-distance call to the mainland from my home.

I had a tremendous support network that always met my doubts with faith. My two boys John and Joey pointed out every rainbow. "Look Mommy, there's a rainbow. That's a promise from God. You'll get those buses." The love and courage so freely shared by my family and friends surrounded me like a warm blanket.

I even called President Mandela's office to learn if he would attend our gala. My heart skipped a beat when the correspondence secretary traced the letter to the deputy director general's office. She remarked: "Oh my, there may be good news for you. They are giving this serious consideration apparently. Your request has been routed to the deputy director general's office. Shall I connect you?"

I swallowed hard and meekly replied: "Yes. Thank you."

Maybe this was the miracle we had been waiting for. How could Roberts Hawaii not give us those buses if the President of South Africa was coming to honor our children? By the time the call was connected to Lois Dippenaar, the assistant to the deputy director general, I was convinced the answer would be a glorious yes. It came as quite a shock to learn he would not be coming. Lois went on and on, gushing about what a lovely project this was and that they had seriously considered our invitation. Unfortunately, President Mandela was exhausted from the state visit of President Clinton. When Lois confided that she used to be an elementary school teacher, I started weeping on the phone.

"Oh, Lois, we don't have buses. The whole event may have to be canceled. That's why I'm calling. I was hoping for a miracle. If President Mandela came, how could they not give us buses? Will you pray for us, Lois?"

"Shelly, of course I will. I will have our whole office pray for you. As you sleep, we will pray. Now go get some rest. It must be very late for you there." With these loving words, a friendship was born. I have never met Lois, but I have spoken with her countless times. I dearly love a woman I have never met, far away in Africa, who always found the time to listen and speak words filled with hope.

Every morning the search would begin all over again. The countdown grew closer: "We are ten days away.… We are nine days away.… We are eight days away…" It was time for drastic measures. I needed a direct line to heaven. I found the phone number for Sister Nirmala in Calcutta, India. She is the Mother General of the Missionaries of Charity. She is Mother Teresa's successor. There was a difference of fifteen and a half hours between Calcutta and Hawaii, so this call had to wait.

I called my parents instead. My mom remarked: "The way things are going, you will probably speak with the Mother General herself." I gasped. My father got on the phone and told me to stop worrying. "Your Auntie Barb has got the prayer line working, and they are not going to quit until you have those buses."

Later that afternoon I called and invited Sister Norise to attend the literacy gala. I had taken a course from Sister Norise the previous summer. Near the end of our conversation I confided to her this final obstacle standing in our path and asked her to pray. She recommended I contact the Augustine Foundation and speak with Tonya Story, the bishop's administrative assistant. "They might be able to help you." I didn't have much confidence that they could help, as I was not having any luck with foundations. But I had to pursue every lead, so I immediately called and spoke with Tonya. She asked me to fax the information to her office and promised to get back to me as soon as possible.

I began complaining to God. "Every time I call a company, God, I'm calling blind. It is so embarrassing. I don't know who to ask for, and I am guessing at their title."

"Could I speak with the CEO, please?"

"You mean the President?"

"Yes, the president. Thank you."

"And this is in reference to …?"

"God, there must be an easier way! There must be a reference book out there. A listing. I am wasting so much valuable time and energy, God, playing this game with the switchboard." As the days drew nearer the deadline, I was becoming more and more irritable.

An hour later the doorbell rang. My neighbor Nancy Moore came bearing a gift and placed it in my hands. "Shelly, I was at the Ewa Beach library book sale, and I had the strangest feeling I should buy this and give it to you. I only spent ten cents. I won't keep you. I have to run and start supper. Hang in there." Then she left.

In my hands I was holding a telephone directory. Only this was the *Hawaii Business Directory 1995.* A little out-of-date, but the information was astonishing. It listed the name and title of the officers of the company, phone number, fax number, and their rating in terms of sales volume. I could work night and day now! I didn't have to call and pitch our project to the secretary in hopes he or she would grant me permission to speak with an executive. To save time I could fax the information to companies and then follow up with a call. Sheepishly I gave thanks to God for His tender care.

I called Calcutta at midnight. It would be 3:30 in the afternoon there. A woman answered and asked me to call back in two hours. The sisters would be returning then. I set my clock for 2:00 a.m. but overslept. When I called and asked to speak with Sister Nirmala, I was advised to call back later. The Mother General was in prayer.

"Oh, okay. But when should I call back?"

"Is this urgent?"

"Oh no, Sister. It's not urgent. It's just that … it's 3:00 a.m. here."

The sister replied: "I see. Just a moment. Can you wait one moment?"

"Of course, Sister. I can wait."

Mother Nirmala was pulled out of prayer to speak to me. I imagine that the sister believed if I was calling at 3:00 a.m., it must be urgent. I walked outside into the night so as not to disturb my family by this late call. Beneath a canopy of stars and moonlight I opened my heart to Sister Nirmala. For the next twenty-three minutes I spoke of my love for Mother Teresa, Kiley Kealoha's tenderness in mass the day I learned Mother had died, the peril facing our school, our intentions to seek God and write a book, and this final mountain standing in our path. "We don't have buses, Sister. I can't find a corporation willing to share the cost. We've come so far. We're so close. I'm afraid."

A warm, loving voice responded on the other side of the world: "You'll get your buses. I'm certain of that. What you must understand is that this is a significant spiritual event. Three hundred lives seeking God together in one day? I am concerned about the children finding Him. I will have my sisters pray that your children find God."

"Oh Sister, thank you. You're absolutely right. If we don't find God there will be no book. I have been so worried about the buses, I didn't even see that mountain. But couldn't you still offer a little prayer for those buses? I would feel so much better knowing you were praying."

"Of course, you have our prayers."

Sister then gave me the fax number of her friend so I could send her the information on our project. Cheerfully I fed the documents into the fax machine, one by one, knowing Sister Nirmala would be receiving these soon on the other end of the world and praying for us.

I slept for a few hours and woke up worried again. We were seven days away… Seven days! In four days I would have to return to school and teach. I was running out of time. Every call I made that day was fraught with desperation. I could no longer hide this from my voice. I was choking back the tears and utter defeat mounting with each "I'm so sorry. Perhaps if you had contacted us sooner." The hours ticked grimly by in this fashion.

Near the end of the day, I received a call from Gail Chew, vice president of marketing for the Hawaii Visitors and Convention Bureau. She asked if I had found anyone interested in sharing the cost of those buses. When I admitted I had found no one, she replied in disbelief: "No one? You have found no one? Do you realize you are seven days away from this event?"

I completely lost my composure. "Dear God! Are you joking? Of course I know that! I am in agony! Do you realize I get up at 3:00 every morning and that is the first thing I think about? I know exactly how close we are to this event, to the day! My every waking moment has been spent in search of this funding."

"Well, who exactly have you called?" she heatedly inquired.

"Do you want the list for today or the total calls made? I have contacted hundreds of companies, Gail! I cannot find one company willing to share the cost. And you call to scold me and ask me if I realize how close we are to failure?"

I couldn't go on. I began weeping.

Gail gently intervened: "Shelly, the reason I am calling is to inform you that the Hawaii Visitors and Convention Bureau is donating a thousand dollars toward the transportation costs. I have already spoken with Sam. This means you only need $3,500 more. You may find that is an easier sum for companies to swallow."

"You are giving us money?" I asked incredulously.

"Well, you sent us a fax requesting money."

I was confused. I had sent them a fax requesting help routing the buses. Then it dawned on me. I wrote my request on the wrong fax sheet. I didn't change the text of the fax! I sent them the fax seeking a transportation partner. A mistake! I had just secured a thousand dollars by mistake! And worse, I had just stormed at her.

"Oh my goodness, Gail. Thank you! I don't know what to say. You are absolutely wonderful! Thank you." I couldn't go on because I was crying again. It was fatigue, grief, endless worry, and joy all rushing in at once.

Gail ended the call by offering some more names I should contact and words of encouragement. "Keep calling. You have your first transportation partner now. Others will follow. Be sure to tell these companies that we have joined this effort."

In celebration, my husband took me out to dinner. I was delighted with this accidental windfall. However, one unsettling fact remained. We still needed $3,500, and I only had one day left of spring break to find the corporate funding.

"Bill, it has taken me weeks to find a thousand dollars. How am I going to find $3,500 dollars—in one day? In reality, I am not any closer," I sighed.

"Shelly, that is simply not true. You've got it, don't you see? Gail is right. You have the Hawaii Visitors and Convention Bureau joining the team. The floodgate has been opened. Other support will pour in. You'll see.

I fell asleep that night dreaming of buses that would not stop to let me board.

Bill woke me with a hot cup of coffee. We were six days away. Six days! Bill was on his way out to catch the boat to Pearl Harbor. He hollered a hasty good-bye. I chased after him, and in the fashion of Scarlett O'Hara I declared with the same conviction, "Bill, as God is my witness, I will not give up. Do you hear me? I will keep calling until the very morning of the event if I have to!"

He cheerfully responded: "You never have to give up. It's called *reschedule*. You have everything else in place. If you need more time to get those buses, then reschedule. I have to run, or I'll miss the boat."

A weight had been lifted by one word: *reschedule*. I could breathe again.

I decided to skip the calls to New York and take a bath. I reread sections of Richard Carlson's book *Don't Worry, Make Money*. I began flipping through the book seeking answers and fell across a passage that spoke straight to my soul. I jumped out of the tub and called Auntie Vangie.

"Vangie! Let me read this to you."

"*…worry and lack of faith are your greatest obstacles. When you take worry out of the picture, your plan will have a chance to unfold. Keep in touch with your sense of knowing, that inner awareness that any goal or dream you have, as long as you know what it is, is within your grasp…. Each hurdle you face and problem you overcome is part of your divine plan.*"

"You see, Vangie? I have been letting fear and worry get in the way! Over what? Time? Oh, for goodnes' sake. Time doesn't mean anything. Not for God. So what if we have six days left? That's plenty of time. Right now we have to maintain complete faith! Our thoughts are powerful, Vangie. They attract exactly what we believe … like a magnet. If two of us believe, the light will be that much brighter. Will you help me, Vangie, by knowing beyond all doubt that we will find the solution?"

"Of course, Shelly!"

"And rather than thinking about all those no's, I should be thinking only of all those who have already helped. And that is everyone, Vangie! Every single executive, unable to offer financial support, has agreed to pray for us. The village has lavished us with their love, prayers, and treasure. With each person I phone I should be speaking from that place of abundance. The generosity of the village is truly awesome, Vangie. And the village is the world!"

"That's right, Shelly. You sound much stronger. Okay then, let's go to work."

Each call made now was filled with love and joy as I invited various companies to join us as a transportation partner. Each call was fun to make. I knew we were close to the answer.

One hour later Vangie called, extremely excited. "You've got it, Shelly. I know it. Call Tonya Story right away."

"Who?"

"Tonya Story from the Augustine Foundation. You've got it!"

I hung up, and the phone rang immediately. It was Tonya Story.

"How is everything going, Shelly? Have you found any corporate sponsors yet?"

"Oh yes! Tonya, the love and support pouring in to this school is breathtaking. Why just yesterday Gail Chew from the Hawaii Visitors and Convention Bureau called to join us as partners."

Tonya interrupted: "Are we too late? The bishop has authorized me to offer the entire amount requested, $4,500. Did we miss our chance?"

With those words I believe I was floating off the ground by at least six inches. A terrible weight had been lifted from me. I felt so light. I quickly replied: "Oh no, Tonya, you're not too late. But we only need $3,500 now to secure the transportation cost."

"Well, you have it. Thank you for asking us. We are so excited for your school."

The minute I hung up the phone I couldn't contain myself for one second more. I jumped up and down, crying and laughing simultaneously. We had made it to the summit. Oh, and it had been such a perilous climb. I kept repeating over and over: "Thank you, God! Oh God, thank you!" I knew where this help truly came from.

I called the school to share the news. "We got it, Vangie! We got the buses!"

Cheers exploded on the other side of the phone as Auntie Vangie relayed this information to everyone in the office. I could hear Auntie Tessie, Miss Cabrera, and Judy Hilario cheering in the background.

"You were right, Vangie. And what's more, Tonya called with the intention of giving us the entire amount we asked for—$4,500! She was even worried they had missed their chance. Can you believe it? My voice and words were so optimistic she believed I already had the funding. And she thanked us for asking them. Isn't that wonderful? Oh Vangie, faith and love move mountains."

Vangie confided why she knew I had the funding. "When Tonya asked for you, Shelly, she asked to speak with Mercy Mecum. That was a sign to me that a miracle was coming. She called you Mercy."

Mercy is Vangie's dearest friend. When Vangie's husband died young and left her all alone to care for their three small children, it was devastating. The most painful time in her day was the hour her husband would typically walk through the door. Vangie would wait for him, knowing he would never come home again. And when the hour passed, she would lay in bed and cry. Mercy, recognizing this

...TOMORROW, MRS. MECUM, WHAT'S GOING TO HAPPEN...?

...WILL EVERYONE BE PUBLISHED...?

particular pain, would visit her friend at 5:00 p.m. and insist they go for a walk. Mercy walked the road of grief beside Vangie every day, without fail, for three years. When the foundation asked by mistake to speak with Mercy Mecum, Vangie knew the search was over.

The days sped by with last-minute preparations. A public address system had to be installed. Tables erected. Tents raised. Parents had to sign 168 permission slips and turn them in within three days. Mrs. Booth, our fifth-grade math teacher, volunteered to track this essential paperwork. The three hundred cameras and notebooks needed labeling. (Miss Felix and Miss Cabrera, the sixth- and seventh-grade teachers, took care of that.) The school sign had to be changed and a banner hung

...DO WE HAVE TO WEAR OUR UNIFORM..?

...WHAT IF WE RUN OUT OF FILM...?

beneath it to mark the moment: "Welcome to our field of dreams. We have left to write a book. We'll be back soon to celebrate." Permission was sought to land the helicopter in the empty field behind the school. The owners were more than happy to allow this. Press releases were drafted and faxed to the media inviting them to witness this extraordinary event. The last-minute questions of the children had to be answered:

"Do we have to wear our uniform?"

"Yes, please wear your uniform. We want to show the world how proud we are of our school."

"Tomorrow, Mrs. Mecum, what's going to happen?"

"Simple, children. Tomorrow the buses will come. We will board different buses and go look for God. We won't know where these buses are going because we want to look only for God every moment of our journey. When you find God, take His picture, and then write about it. People are very interested to know where you find God, children. So with your photographs and writing a publisher will make a book. Someday people all over the world will read your words and admire your photographs."

"What if we run out of film early? What should we do?"

"Keep writing, even if you run out of film. It may be the very last thing you write that will be published."

"Will everyone be published?"

"No, children. But everyone will have a chance to become published authors. That's what all writers face, children. They write their very best and send it to a publisher and hope and pray an editor likes it enough to make a book. But many times that answer is no. So if this is your dream, you must keep writing and practicing and sending your work to many publishers. Then one day you may open your mail and find that an editor loves your work enough to make a book. You have been granted the opportunity of a lifetime. You may become an author. Just like a real writer, your work will be read by a publisher for possible publication. Do your best. You are ready!"

The children's jitters had to be soothed:

"Yes, you can do this!"

"Yes, you'll find God."

"How do I know? Because the sisters in Calcutta are praying for you. They are praying you will find God. Children, their prayers go straight to heaven, because their lives of service are a perfect form of prayer."

When the children learned I drew courage and comfort from the song "I Believe I Can Fly" by R. Kelly, the fourth- and the sixth-grade students sang this song to me as a present:

Marco Corpuz, age 10

There are miracles in life I must achieve
But first I know it starts inside of me
If I can see it, then I can be it
If I just believe it, there's nothing to it
I believe I can fly
I believe I can touch the sky
I think about it every night and day
Spread my wings then fly away
I believe I can soar
I see me running through that open door
I believe I can fly

And across the field, as the children sang, I locked eyes with Travis Moi, an eighth-grade boy. He stopped in his tracks, flapped his arms as if in flight, and reached up to touch the sky, then waved to me. Oh, the children and their tender ways! What a gift from heaven to be their teacher.

The last evening was spent transforming our school grounds into a "field of dreams." It was as if the conch shell had been blown, summoning the village. The community poured in to help. Teachers, children, and parents painted beautiful banners and hung them all over the campus. The office became a floral shop. The refrigerator that typically chilled soda pop was storing beautiful exotic flowers. Elaborate centerpieces and flower arrangements were molded and designed by the artistic efforts of our librarian, Shirley Castro; our kindergarten teacher, Brenda Levy; and her friends Pat, Debbie, and Robin. Leis for the dignitaries coming to welcome our new authors home were strung patiently by Tesha and Grandma Malama, Thelma Parish, and Anita and Theresa Gonzalves. Auntie Vangie and Fred Gonzales transformed the seventh-grade classroom into a banquet hall. They all worked long into the night. Then, one by one, the village went home to rest, weary from their labors of love.

The transformation of the school grounds was complete. It was a wonderland of colors. Six weeks of tears, worry, wonder, laughter, prayers, faith, hope, and love taught us all, young and old alike.

We can fly! When the morning comes, we will begin our quest.

Kaena Point
Mokuleia Beach
Sunset Beach
Waimea Bay
Pu'uomahuka Heiau
Haleiwa
Schofield Barracks
Wahiawa
Makaha
Waianae
Mililani
Nanakuli
Waikele
Pearl City
A
Pearl Harbor
Ford Island
Barbers Point
EWA BEACH
Honolulu Int'l Airport
Sa
A
Fa

Prologue

THE JOURNEY: "THE BEST FOR THE BEST"

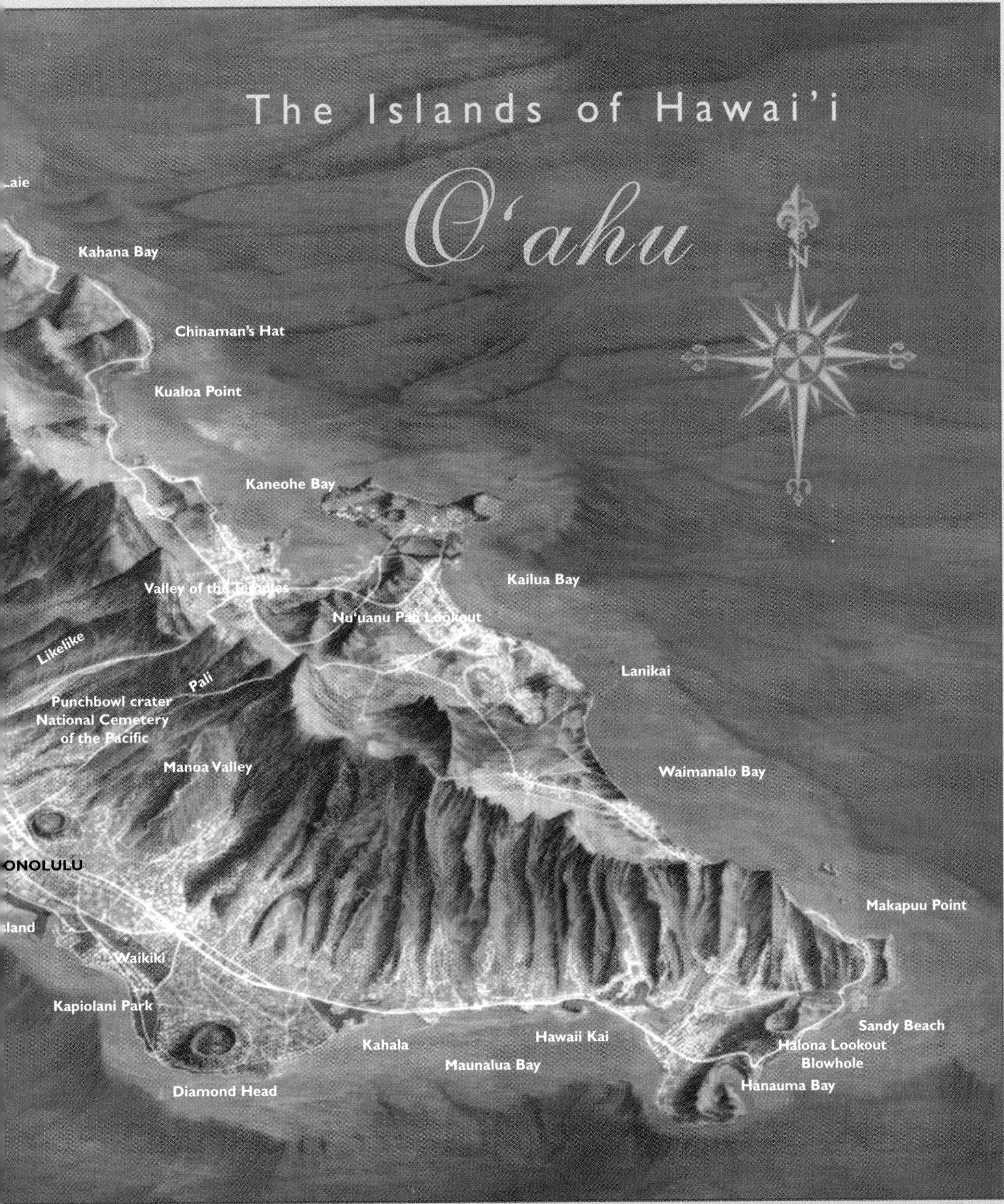
The Islands of Hawai'i
O'ahu
N
Laie
Kahana Bay
Chinaman's Hat
Kualoa Point
Kaneohe Bay
Kailua Bay
Valley of the Temples
Nu'uanu Pali Lookout
Likelike
Pali
Lanikai
Punchbowl crater
National Cemetery
of the Pacific
Manoa Valley
Waimanalo Bay
ONOLULU
Makapuu Point
sland
Waikiki
Kapiolani Park
Sandy Beach
Halona Lookout
Blowhole
Kahala
Hawaii Kai
Maunalua Bay
Hanauma Bay
Diamond Head

The Art Map of Oahu, Hawaii", watercolor painting by Gary Hincks © Claremark Ltd

Rose Oasay, grandmother, age 69

OUR LADY OF PERPETUAL HELP SCHOOL GROUNDS.
CHILDREN, PARENTS, GRANDPARENTS, STAY IN LINE AS THEY WAIT TO SEEK GOD.
WHEREVER THEY GO-AMAZING GRACE.

Liliy Lambinico, grandmother, age 64

THE DAY BEGINS WITH AN AWE-INSPIRING VISION OF FOURTEEN LUXURY MOTOR-COACHES PULLING INTO THE SMALL PARKING LOT FRONTING OUR LADY OF PERPETUAL HELP SCHOOL. EARLIER, MANY EWA RESIDENTS WERE STARTLED BY THE SIGHT OF THIS MAGNIFICENT CONVOY HEADING TOWARDS THEM AS THEY MADE THEIR WAY WEARILY TO WORK IN TOWN. IMAGINE! FOURTEEN LUXURY TOUR BUSES DRIVING IN A CARAVAN ON A FREEWAY, HEADING FOR A LITTLE SCHOOL, WAY OUT IN THE COUNTRY.

The school community is spellbound as the first of the great buses pulls into the driveway, followed closely by a second, a third, a fourth, a fifth. There is no end in sight to these buses turning into the driveway of our little school. We stand transfixed and stare in wonderment with huge smiles on our faces. Laughter fills the air. The children jump up and down joyfully, some turn cartwheels. Will there be enough concrete to temporarily park these luxury motor coaches, seen typically in Waikiki, never in Ewa Beach? Are we dreaming?

I SAW GOD IN UNCLE BILL, OUR BUS DRIVER. HE IS SO NICE TO US. HE TOOK US TO THIS PLACE SAFE.

Elvin Ray Vitug, age 6

Elvin Ray Vitug

Lourdes Cabinatan, mother, age 62

THE BUS IS A SYMBOL OF GOD, HE IS GUIDING US TO EVERY PLACE WE ARE GOING- THAT WE MAY BE SAFE AND SOUND.

Julia Cabinatan, age 15

Shane Duhon, age 26

Mary Ellen Miller, teacher, age 47

GUY,
OUR BUSDRIVER.
HE HAS THE GIFT
OF SUNSHINE,
A PHYSICAL
WARMTH TO LET
US FEEL GOD'S
LOVE.

Shane Duhon, age 26

Remedios Cabrera, age 52

Most of us stare in silence at a miracle unfolding before our very eyes, as each gargantuan coach pulls into the driveway and finds a place to stop and wait for us to board. The sound of engines idling and the smell of diesel fuel fill the air. When all buses have found their place to park, the engines are suddenly cut and an expectant quiet wafts over the assembly. The bus drivers climb down and stand near one another talking quietly and joking amongst themselves.

The bus drivers are genuinely delighted to see us. Each has been given his assigned route, as well as a copy of the Honolulu Star Bulletin article detailing our dream for the children and their families. They are rooting for us. Some drivers have taken the time to make signs, which they hang on the

SO MANY
ROADS TO TAKE
AND YOU LET US
MAKE THE
CHOICE.

Julia Chun, grandmother, age 65

Julia Chun

side of their buses as a greeting: "The Best For the Best." We all feel a bit like Cinderella going to our first ball, and our coaches are awaiting us.

When we enter the school grounds, our names are checked against a roster. We are assigned a number from one to fourteen. We stand in a line with others holding the same number. This is our bus assignment. Our destination? This remains a closely guarded secret. Only two people on each bus are privy to this information: the bus driver and a teacher in charge of that group.

The teachers stand at the head of the line, behind numbered orange cones, guiding the bemused children and adults to their starting places. News reporters from both print and television media stand to the side taking notes, photographs, and filming the gathering. This whole adventure has had an unreal dream-like quality-- until the arrival of those buses. Now we know we are wide awake and this is real.

Holden Moi

Father Bob holds a megaphone to his mouth and invites us to pray. We bow our heads and allow the words barked through a megaphone to stir through our hearts, and whisper to our souls, an unspoken invitation: "Come seek me." After the final blessing, we board our respective luxury motor coaches. Our journey begins!

All fourteen buses start their engines in unison and pull out of the driveway, one by one. The buses stay close together in a caravan until they reach the freeway. Then they begin to part company, heading off in opposite directions. Still, a sizable number of buses are traveling into town together. One by one, each bus takes a different exit ramp, till all motor coaches are traveling alone, utterly alone, on their own spiritual quest.

I SEE GOD IN THE BUS DRIVER BECAUSE HE DOES MANY GOOD DEEDS.

Holden Moi, age 10

I SAW GOD IN THE
BUS BECAUSE HE IS
EVERYWHERE.

Reisha Alcain, age 7

Leslie Aguinaldo, age 13

CARS REMIND ME
OF HOW GOD
TRAVELS FROM
HEART TO HEART,
ALWAYS FORGIVING.

Coca Te'Moananui, age 12

Shane Duhon, age 26

Chapter 1

"I SEE GOD UP IN THE PALM TREE SINGING"

Briana Conway, age 6

Barbara Hernandez, age 13

Christopher Cruz, age 10

THE MOUNTAIN IS POINTING AT GOD.

Jacob Aplaca, age 6

Bus Number One heads for the windward side of the island. Its first stop is the Nuuanu Pali Lookout. The windward side of the island is so called for the prevailing cloud-laden westerly trade winds that blow in from the ocean and stack up against the Koolau Range, unloading misty rains. Rainbows dazzle the eyes here.

From a V-shaped crack, the Pali Lookout provides sweeping vistas of the almost perpendicular fluted cliffs of the green Koolaus, which stretch from the northern to the southern tips of the island, down to the tropically lush valleys two and three thousand feet below and across a verdant plain to the distant ocean. The winds can blow here with such force that walking is difficult. Eight-year-old Sarah Espiritu's pen is blown right out of her hand as she writes in her notebook. A mother reaches deep into her purse and hands her a spare one.

Wade Abendanio, age 11

Sarah Espiritu

Sarah Espiritu

GOD BLOWS
AND MAKES
WAVES.

Sarah Espiritu, age 8

GOD LIKES TO
SWIM, HE LIKES
TO BE SEEN
BY PEOPLE.

Sarah Espiritu

From there the bus winds steeply down to Kailua town to stop for a moment at Kailua Beach. The shade from the ironwood trees at the edge of the powdery white sandy shores provides respite from the burning rays of the sun. Many windsurfers frequent this beach to take advantage of the frequent gusty onshore winds. This beach is equally popular with families because of the safe swimming.

Next they travel to the secluded community of Lanikai, with its breathtaking view of the uninhabited Moku Lua Islands. These two islands serve as bird sanctuaries. The water is calm here as well, protected by reefs offshore.

The last stop is the Valley of the Temples, home of the Byoda-In Temple, an exact replica of the Byoda-In Temple built nine hundred years ago in Uji, Japan. On the drive in, the bus passes a cemetery

GOD MADE PINK FLOWERS TO MAKE ME HAPPY.
Jacob Aplaca, age 6

Mark Ornellas, father, age 36

Anthony Souza, father, age 45

I TOOK A PICTURE OF MY BROTHER BECAUSE I LOVE HIM, AND GOD IS LOVE.
Briana Conway, age 6

laid out on wide-open grassy hills. The serenity of the koi ponds, temple bell, waterfalls, peacocks and the striking curtain of the Koolau Mountain Range transport all visitors to another time and place.

Bus One seeks God in these tranquil locations. And God is found. The children and their families find God actively participating in our world in many surprising ways. On this day, God leads an ambulance to safety. He walks the beaches ensuring that no one drowns. He gives life, takes life, and guides each soul in between. He sculpts nature into interesting designs as He continues to create worlds within worlds. He tenderly feeds a peacock and is concerned with His creature's happiness. God helps the newborn fish swim through the waves as He helps us swim through life. God likes to swim and be seen, blow and make waves, and grow palm trees tall. He is heard making lots of noise in the form of a bell. God is seen up in a palm tree—singing.

Yes, God is busy in our world. Yet He is not too busy to create pink flowers just to make one little boy happy.

Heather Hauhio

I TOOK A PICTURE OF THE TEMPLE
AND GOD IS IN IT.

Heather Hauhio, age 5

Kellie Hauhio, mother, age 27

IN THE TEMPLE I
SMELL INCENSE,
AND GOD WAS
THERE WITH US.

Anita Ginoza, mother, age 42

Nicole Cadile, age 12

I SAW GOD BY THE PEACOCK.
HE WAS FEEDING IT LOTS OF FOOD AND
ASKING: "ARE YOU HAPPY?"

Victoria Souza, age 8

Chapter 2

"HE IS THE ROCK"

Ashley Wilhelm, age 5

Maris Corpuz, age 9

Marco Corpuz, age 10

WAVES! WAVES! WAVES!
THEY'RE ALL AROUND THE ISLAND POUNDING AGAINST THE MOUNTAINS!
GOD'S LOVE SURROUNDS US ALL.

Irma Bajar, age 20

THE CHILDREN AND THEIR FAMILIES ABOARD BUS TWO ARE UNAWARE THAT THEY ARE IN FOR A DELICIOUS VISUAL SERVING OF OAHU'S FAMOUS SOUTHERN SHORES. THE BUS HUGS THE WINDING COASTAL HIGHWAY AND PULLS INTO AS MANY OVERLOOKS AS CAN BE SAFELY MANAGED, GIVEN THE SIZE OF THE VEHICLE AND THE WIDTH OF THE ROAD.

Many lives have been lost along this coastline. The waves can be unfriendly, even dangerous to those who turn their backs on the ocean here. So the children and their families cling to one another as they witness one of nature's wilder shores.

Jordan Barlan Mattson, age 6

I SEE GOD IN THE OCEAN BECAUSE THAT'S THE AMOUNT OF LOVE HE'S GIVEN US.

Keala Lee

Ashley Wilhelm, age 5

I SEE GOD IN THOSE TREES BECAUSE THEY LOOK LIKE A CLOSE FAMILY. GOD TO ME IS A CLOSE FAMILY MEMBER.

Keala Lee, age 12

Jordan Barlan Mattson, age 6

I SEE GOD IN THE BLOWHOLE BECAUSE I SEE HIM PRAYING IN THE ROCKS. HE RAISES HIS HAND AND THERE IS AIR AND WIND AND WAVES COMING TO GOD.

Marco Corpuz, age 10

I SAW THIS BEAUTIFUL ROCK. IT LOOKED LIKE GOD WAS IN IT.

Jacob Butler, age 5

Linda Sullivan, mother, age 40

I FOUND GOD IN THESE CHILDREN PLAYING HAPPILY AND INNOCENTLY TOGETHER.

Mirasol Corpuz, mother, age 44

Remedios Cabrera, teacher, age 52

After a long peaceful ride on an "interstate" past Honolulu, the bus rolls down the handsomely landscaped Kalanianaole Highway for its first stop at Maunalua Bay. Coconut palms trace the deserted beach and the shallow water covering mudflats and coral. The outer reef breaks the deep ocean in long curves of whitecapped waves. After taking a few moments to stretch and play with the rocks, they continue up the flank of Koko Head to Hanauma Bay. This is a tourist hot spot, and the bus driver has to compete with other buses for parking. People are drawn here from around the world to snorkel in this brilliant shallow bay, cut into the side of an extinct volcano. There is a steep walkway down, with a view far below of the turquoise waters in the perfect sandy cove, coral reefs, and hordes of swimmers. Many snorkelers purchase fish food to attract schools of exotic tropical fish that nibble from their hands. It's like swimming in an enormous fishbowl. Elvis Presley's *Blue Hawaii* was filmed here.

Wilton Wilhelm, father, age 27

I SEE GOD ON THE MOUNTAIN, IN THE SKY, IN THE OCEAN,
AND ON THE CLIFF. WHEREVER I GO I SEE GOD.

Maris Corpuz, age 9

On this day, however, the tourists are more interested in observing our families as they seek God. The tourists are quite surprised to see the giant motor coach pull up bearing uniform-clad schoolchildren. When Miss Cabrera shares the vision with these visitors, they are deeply moved. As the children and their families turn their cameras to take pictures of God, the tourists take photos of the God-seekers.

The next two stops feature the Halona Coast as it rounds the steep, deeply eroded slopes of

Remedios Cabrera, teacher, age 52

WE CAN LOOK FOR GOD
STANDING ON THE ROCKS.
WE CAN SEEK GOD HERE
BECAUSE THE ROCKS LOOK
DIFFERENT AND GOD'S POWER
AND CREATION MADE THEM

Maris Corpuz

Remedios Cabrera

Koko Head Crater, another extinct volcano. First the bus pulls over at the Halona Lookout, where on a clear day the islands of Molokai, Lanai, and Maui can be seen thirty miles and further across the blue ocean. Next is the Halona Blowhole. Here wind, waves, and rocks work together to provide a spectacular water show. If all of the elements are in sync, a towering waterspout will shoot up from a rough hole in the lava bench. The spume may spray the startled visitors above.

Angelica Juanillo

WE COME TO THIS PARK WHERE THERE ARE
SWINGS, SLIDES, A LADDER, AND A BASKETBALL COURT.
I THINK GOD IS HERE WATCHING OVER US EVEN AS WE LIVE.

Angelica Juanillo, age 9

The children and families stop for lunch at Sandy Beach, popularly known as Broken Neck Beach, probably the most dangerous beach on Oahu. The shorebreak pounds down on coral flats, and dangerous rip tides run offshore and out to sea. However, these very challenges lure daredevil bodysurfers to its perilous shores.

The final stop is Makapuu Point. From here our children and families look across at uninhabited Rabbit Island and the smaller Turtle Island. Both are bird sanctuaries. The majestic view of the windward coast sweeps up the vertical cliffs of the Koolau Mountain Range behind, past the three needle peaks of lonely Olomana. Hang gliders hover and swoop above as our children and families hike down to Little Makapuu Beach to enjoy the tide pools filled with life.

Keala Lee

HAVE YOU EVER WONDERED HOW MUCH SAND THERE IS IN THE WORLD? I
BET THERE IS THE SAME AMOUNT OF PEOPLE THAT THERE IS OF SAND.
ONE PERSON HE MADE IS KEALA.

Keala Lee, age 12

As nine-year-old Angelica Juanillo spends the day beside her father gazing at the wild beauty of these southern shores, she senses the presence of her mother hovering above her. Angelica lost her mother, Ester, at the tender age of five. This is not the first time she has felt her mother's presence. No, little Angelica affirms that her mother comes to her each night before she falls asleep. But this day is different. On this day, a family is reunited. Bathed in the undying love of her mother and father, Angelica finds God.

This journey takes the seekers to the natural beauty of the southern shores of Oahu. And God is found. God continues to shape and create a lovely world, rich in colors, shapes, and textures. Why? Perhaps, as one of our mothers muses, He indeed intends for us to be delighted. Nonetheless, all agree that God makes this world so beautiful simply because He loves us.

Chapter 3

"I Have Learned That God Lives in the Hard Rock Cafe"

Deyandra Abella, age 5

Beth Hannes, mother, age 37

I SEE
GOD IN
THE SKY
IN WAIKIKI.

Jill Hannes, age 10

Jill Hannes

THE CHILDREN, THE FAMILIES, AND OUR PRINCIPAL, MR. SASAKI, BOARD BUS THREE. THERE ARE LAST-MINUTE FAMILY MEMBERS JOINING THIS JOURNEY. SOME OF OUR PARENTS ARE UNSURE IF THEIR WORK WILL ALLOW THEM THE TIME OFF. WE HAVE PLANNED FOR THIS BY HAVING EXTRA NOTEBOOKS ON EACH BUS. MR. SASAKI, HOWEVER, IS FACED WITH AN IMMEDIATE DECISION WHEN THIS BUS LEAVES THE SCHOOL GROUNDS. They are short one camera and one notebook. He makes his decision quietly and secretly. He gives his camera and notebook away to a mother. And no one notices this small act of love.

*"Where God is, there is love; and where there is love,
there always is an openness to serve."*—Mother Teresa

So begins the journey in search of God for Bus Three.

They are heading for a different world: Waikiki, a world of high-rise hotels and condos, shopping plazas that sell everything from sandals, sarongs, and sun lotion to paintings and sculptures priced in the six figures. A boardwalk spans the length of the beach of sticky golden sand from Kapiolani Park at the Diamond Head end to the Ala Wai Yacht Basin at the other. Melodic Hawaiian music flows through the grand hotel lobbies.

Edona Queja, mother, age 33

GOD IS THE INSPIRATION TO
DO WHATEVER YOU ARE DOING.
HE GIVES YOU IDEAS.

Leslie Aguinaldo, age 13

CONSTRUCTION-GOD LOVES
CONTRUCTION.

Landon Aano, age 6

I SAW THAT THE
BIG STATUE IS
SMALLER THAN
GOD.

Deyandra Abella, age 5

Pete Veglak, father, age 34

Pete Veglak

Edona Queja

Kevin Hannes, father, age 36

I LIKE TO WATCH THE
WAVES DANCING WITH GOD.

Deyandra Abella, age 5

I SEE GOD IN THE WATER WITH
PEOPLE PLAYING AND HAVING FUN.

Jill Hannes, age 10

RIDING THE TROLLEY IS A GOOD WAY
TO MEET PEOPLE WHILE LOOKING
FOR HIM.

Edona Queja, mother, age 33

Pete Veglak

GOD HELPS US REMEMBER OUR HEROES WITH A SIMPLE STRAND OF FLOWERS.

Pete Veglak, father, age 34

Irene Alcain

I SEE GOD IN THE FOOD THAT WE EAT.

Irene Alcain, mother, age 33

Our families stroll about and drink in the sights and sounds typically enjoyed by tourists who come from all over the world. They walk the beaches, hotel lobbies, and shopping pavilions with the same awe and wonder as the visitors to our island. They are given a pass to ride the Waikiki Trolley at their leisure. The trolley shuttles passengers between the major landmarks of Waikiki and downtown Honolulu. With an all-day pass, our families are able to get off wherever the inspiration moves them and then board another trolley to continue on their journey. This is a real treat, for many have never even played tourist in their own backyard.

Carlo Barbasa

THE POWER OF
GOD AND THE
HEAVENS HAVE
KEPT THIS GLASS
BUILDING STANDING.

Carlo Barbasa, age 12

Kyle Villanueva

I SAW MISS UNIVERSE IN THE HOTEL
LOBBY WITH GOD.

Deyandra Abella, age 5

QUEEN LILI'UOKALANI
OWNED THE ISLAND OF OAHU.
GOD MADE HER TO BE QUEEN OF OAHU.
NOW SHE IS WITH GOD IN HEAVEN.
I SEE GOD IN THIS STATUE.

Kyle Villanueva, age 9

Genefred Cruz, age 9

Grandmother Sophie Sambueno has never ridden the trolley. The moment she steps aboard she is flooded with a memory from her childhood. She remembers standing with her parents on a street corner, waiting to catch a glimpse of the trolley transporting the legendary child-star Shirley Temple through the streets of Waikiki. Little Sophie waved to Shirley Temple as the trolley sped past. Grandmother Sophie smiles at the memory as she settles into her seat.

The children and their families explore downtown Honolulu. Towering skyscrapers, the State Capitol, and the Aloha Tower are but a few of the landmarks they encounter. This group reunites at the *Falls of Clyde*, a beautifully maintained square-rigger from Hawaii's early sailing days.

Kyle Villanueva

Lunch is a picnic on Magic Island, overlooking a beautiful marina. Yachts, outrigger canoes, and surfers serve up a visual treat for our families as they sit beneath shady trees to eat.

Our families seek God in these ordinary places. However, when God is found, places do not remain ordinary. No, soon the veil is lifted to reveal the extraordinary. On this day, God gifts the families with a singular blessing. They see their island with the vision of a child.

I SEE GOD IN THIS
SHIP BECAUSE IT'S
VERY OLD AND HAS
NEVER SUNK YET
AND IT'S STILL
STRONG.

Kyle Villanueva, age 9

Deyandra Abella, age 5

GOD KEEPS US
AFLOAT
THROUGH ALL
OUR PROBLEMS.

Nina Barbasa, mother, age 45

Pete Veglak

GOD IS IN A HANDFUL OF BREAD CRUMBS.

Pete Veglak, father, age 34

Chapter 4

"God Is Here
Taking Care of the Living and the Dead"

Elvin Ray Vitug, age 6

Barbara Hernandez, age 13

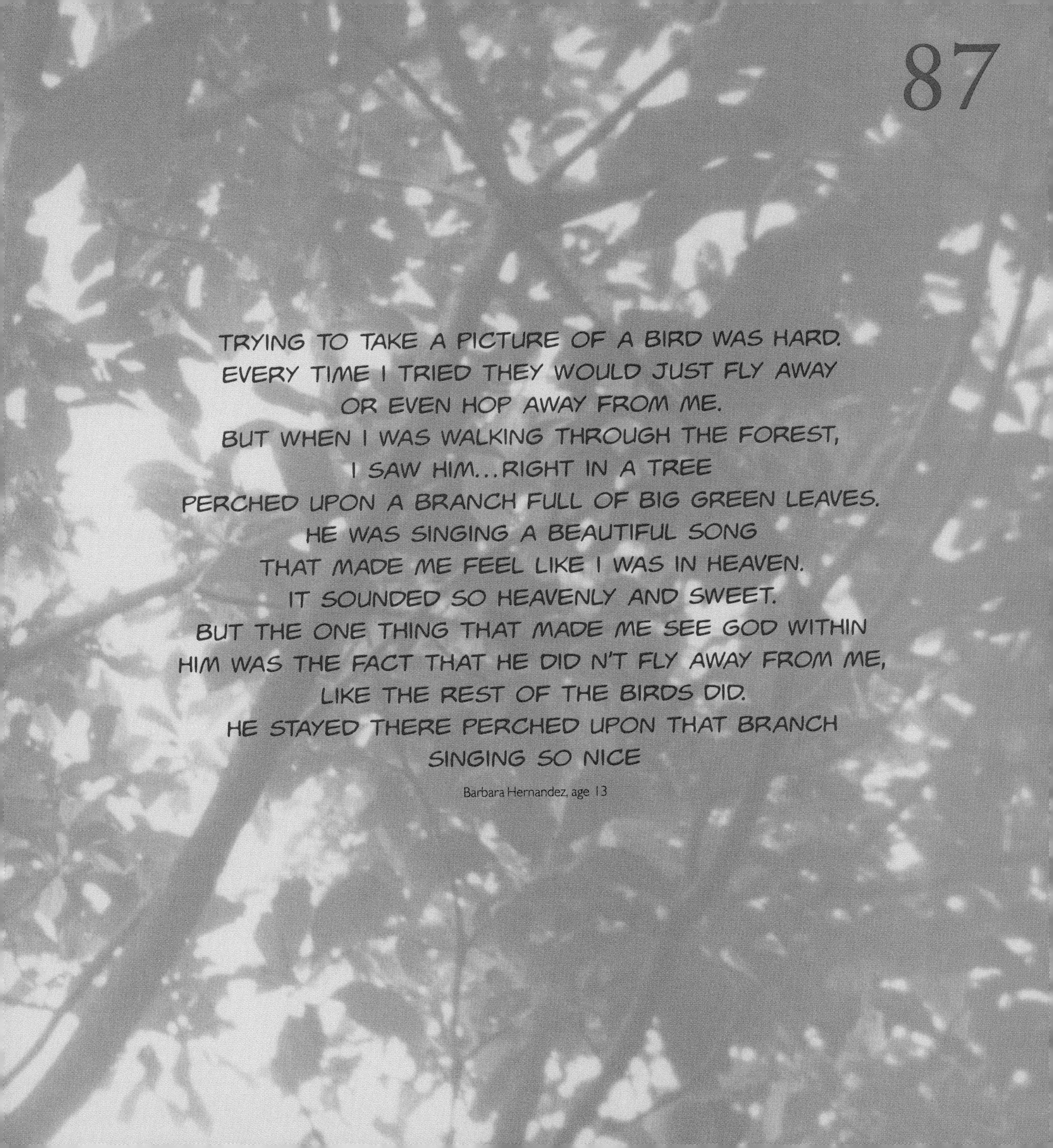

TRYING TO TAKE A PICTURE OF A BIRD WAS HARD.
EVERY TIME I TRIED THEY WOULD JUST FLY AWAY
OR EVEN HOP AWAY FROM ME.
BUT WHEN I WAS WALKING THROUGH THE FOREST,
I SAW HIM...RIGHT IN A TREE
PERCHED UPON A BRANCH FULL OF BIG GREEN LEAVES.
HE WAS SINGING A BEAUTIFUL SONG
THAT MADE ME FEEL LIKE I WAS IN HEAVEN.
IT SOUNDED SO HEAVENLY AND SWEET.
BUT THE ONE THING THAT MADE ME SEE GOD WITHIN
HIM WAS THE FACT THAT HE DID N'T FLY AWAY FROM ME,
LIKE THE REST OF THE BIRDS DID.
HE STAYED THERE PERCHED UPON THAT BRANCH
SINGING SO NICE

Barbara Hernandez, age 13

Barbara Hernandez, age 13

Bus Number Four drives town-bound on H-1 until the University exit for Manoa Valley. It passes through the wide lower valley that cradles the campus, then winds up to the head of the valley. Looking back over the dense pattern of houses, the passengers see the distant towers of bustling Waikiki silhouetted against the ocean horizon. The families stop at Paradise Park to rest and explore the serene outer gardens under the canopy of the immense trees of a lush tropical rain forest. There is a deep living silence here, broken only by the songs of birds and the fall of each footstep.

From here the families travel to Punchbowl Crater to visit the National Memorial Cemetery of the Pacific. This extinct volcano serves as the final resting place for more than thirty thousand of this nation's war heroes. Buried here is Ellison Onizuka, Hawaii's astronaut killed in the 1986 explosion of the space shuttle *Challenger*. Buried here is a husband and beloved father. Puowaina, which translates literally as "Hill of Sacrifice," is the Hawaiian name for this sacred place.

Donna Bell

Julia Hernandez

THE WHITE FLOWERS ARE SPECIAL BECAUSE GOD CREATED EACH ONE. AND THAT FLOWER WAS SPECIAL TO ME AND GOD.

Julia Hernandez, age 6

I FOUND GOD IN A FLOWER. IT WAS DARK PINK, YELLOW, AND ORANGE. IT WAS FLOATING IN A POND WITH A WATERFALL.

Donna Bell, age 9

I SEE GOD IN THE GREAT VINES. HE HANGS THERE BECAUSE HE IS STRONG.

Jason DeGuzman, age 11

Melody Baldonado

Elvin Ray Vitug, age 6

I SEE GOD IN WATERFALLS BECAUSE HE WASHES HIS FEET.

Melody Baldonado, age 7

Mark Deus, age 9

PUNCHBOWL CEMETERY. THIS IS A PLACE WHERE GOD IS MOST OF THE TIME. THIS IS A PLACE WHERE YOU HAVE TO RESPECT GOD AND THE PEOPLE BURIED HERE.

Davin Dionisio, age 13

I TOOK A PICTURE OF AN ARMY STANDING WITH GOD.

Gladys Gamaio, age 10

David Moore

Evangeline Dionisio, mother, age 49

THE PASSING OF A SOUL FROM US TO HIM.

David Moore, father, age 38

GODS LOVE IS
BOUNDLESS.
ULTIMATE
LOVE AND
VISION
DEFINES AN
ULTIMATE
HERO.

Joey Mapanao, father, age 38

Donna Bell, age 9

I SAW GOD HERE, BECAUSE LOVE BETWEEN LIFE AND DEATH IS SPECIAL.

Stephanie Closson, age 13

Elvin Ray Vitug, age 6

One mother is quite startled to learn she has been brought here. Evangeline Dionisio has not walked these slopes and sweeping lawns with their flat stone markers since the day she buried her husband, the father of her young children, nearly eleven years ago. God walks beside Evangeline and her son Davin, and there is peace.

The next stop is Cannery Row in the industrial heart of the city. The families browse in the boutiques and stores built inside the extinct pineapple processing factory. From there they cross Sand Island to the quiet local beach where they can watch the Coast Guard boats in Honolulu Harbor sail in and out, on their mission to save lives. Sailboats glide by, a soothing visual respite from the traffic of the city. The families enjoy a picnic and walk the shoreline before they board again to return to school.

The children and their families search for God in these serene and somber locations, and God is found tenderly caring for both the living and the dead. God cares for all His living creatures—from the birds so vulnerable and frail yet brave in flight and song to the blossoms that raise their shining faces to us in complete beauty. God loves and tenderly cares for His flowers—especially those cut too soon from the stem of life—who gave their lives to save the lives of others, heroes who lie quietly in rest in the floor of Punchbowl Crater. God comforts all hearts, especially the hearts of a mother and her son who walk yet in grief.

At the close of this day spent in search of Him, the children note the footprints in the sand. Yes, God walks beside us every step of the way, along garden paths, on cemetery hills, in tourist shops, and on ocean-lapped beaches. We never walk alone.

GOD MADE ME AND MY FRIENDS.

Mark Deus, age 9

Joey Mapanao, father, age 38

THEY DIED FOR OUR COUNTRY. NOW GOD WILL BE WITH THEM ALWAYS.

Antoinette Algono, mother, age 29

Jason DeGuzman, age 11

I THINK GOD MADE WAVES TO HELP CLEAN THE BEACHES.

Davin Dionisio, age 13

Mark Deus

GOD SAID, "SIT UNDER THE COCONUT TREE AND REST."

Rose Oasay, grandmother, age 69

Buenaventurada Canubida, grandmother, age 79

Chapter 5

"GOD'S LOVELY DREAMS FOR THE FUTURE"

Jessica Fernandez, age 10

Elizabeth Fall,
HarperCollins

I SAW GOD IN THE MOUNTAINS AND I
FELT HIM TOUCHING MY HAND.

Merebel Garcia, age 8

Zachary Ajifu, age 9

Janinne Jurin, teacher, age 28

B US FIVE IS IN FOR A TREAT. THEY ARE ON THEIR WAY TO ONE OF THE WORLD'S MOST RECOGNIZABLE NATURAL LANDMARKS—DIAMOND HEAD, LOOMING OVER WAIKIKI. AFTER PASSING THROUGH THE TUNNEL INTO THE BONE-DRY CRATER THE FAMILIES BRAVE THE HIKE UP TO THE RIM. OF COURSE, THE JOURNEY IS NOT AN EASY ONE. THERE IS ONE SECTION WHERE THEY MUST CLIMB NINETY-NINE STEEP STEPS AND MOUNT A WINDING STAIRCASE IN THE DARK (SAVE FOR THOSE SOULS WHO COME PREPARED WITH A FLASHLIGHT). Along the way they pass old bunkers, souvenirs of World War II. Once at the top, a gorgeous breeze cools every head, and children, parents, and grandparents are rewarded with a stunning panoramic view that leaves them breathless. They see Waikiki and the southern shores of Oahu from the heavens.

Landon Aano, age 6

GOD IS GIVING
HIS PEOPLE
STRENGTH
TO BE AS
HIGH AS HIM.

Jessica Fernandez, age 10

THERE YOU ARE GOD,
WAY UP ON TOP OF DIAMOND HEAD.
I ONLY MEET YOU HALF WAY UP.

Julia Chun, grandmother, age 65

Winifred Largo

Hattie Santos, grandmother, age 72

GOD IS HERE IN THE PEOPLE OF ALL
RACES, LIVING IN HARMONY.

Winifred Largo, grandmother, age 56

THE LIGHTHOUSE IS
JUST LIKE GOD.
IT SHINES LIGHT TO
BOATS AND SHIPS AS
GOD SHINES ON
EVERYONE.

Fitzgerald Fuentes, age 13

Janinne Jurin, teacher, age 28

I TOOK A PICTURE OF THE LIGHTHOUSE
BECAUSE GOD ALWAYS LIGHTS THE WAY
TO HEAVEN.

Patrick Aano, age 12

Kimberley Ben, age 5

Diamond Head proves to be quite a challenging climb for fourteen-year-old Julia Alcartado. As she climbs the "rugged, rough hard trail and steps," Julia senses the presence of God. Words of encouragement wash over her at the very moment she is ready to admit defeat. "Come on, Lia. You can make it. Don't give up." And Julia continues to climb until she makes it to the very top of Diamond Head.

This is not the first mountain this tender teenager has had to scale. Earlier in the school year Julia began the daunting process of becoming a United States citizen. The final challenge was a fearsome interview with the Department of Immigrations. Yet God sends nothing less than angels when His children are afraid. Julia received a letter from the First Lady on the very day she had to endure her final interview. Standing beside her mother, with her friends and teacher encircling her, Julia wept on the playground as she tried to read aloud these words of encouragement. She couldn't finish the letter. She passed the letter to me, her teacher. "Can I continue to read aloud, Julia?" With her hands covering her face she nodded.

I hope that you will continue to work hard in school and to take part in community service activities. You have my best wishes for a bright future filled with happiness and much success.
Sincerely yours, Hillary Rodham Clinton

Later, at Immigrations, Julia's mother presented this letter to the official who would be determining her daughter's fate. He silently read, then looked up and said, "Well, I think this answers all of my questions." That very day Julia officially became a citizen of the United States.

The next stop, Diamond Head Lighthouse, one of the oldest operational lighthouses in the United States, is in clear sight right below them. Our families descend the steep staircase cautiously, enthusiastically greeting and encouraging those who are making the laborious ascent. They climb back into their bus, and their driver guides them out through the crater wall again and around the

I SEE GOD IN THE BEAUTIFUL CHANDELIERS OF THE KAHALA MANDARIN ORIENTAL HOTEL.

Hattie Santos, grandmother, age 72

Lourdes Cabinatan, mother, age 52

Hattie Santos

Miles Ajifu, father, age 38

DOLPHINS ARE GOD'S PETS.

Lucia Fuentes, mother, age 30

base of the volcano toward the lighthouse. The cliff-top park here is one of the island's most popular spots, a place where tourists and locals alike come to sit on the wall to watch the acrobatic windsurfers and drink in the endless sea that all but swallows the sun as it sets.

Next is the Kahala Mandarin Oriental Hotel, tucked away in the chic multimillion-dollar oceanfront estates of Kahala, where our families enjoy a free dolphin show. The three dolphins have

WHEN TWO
OR THREE
ARE GATHERED,
YOU ARE IN THE
MIDST.

Julia Chun, grandmother, age 65

Julia Chun

Jessica Fernandez

GOD IS LETTING
HIM GO TO PEACE.

Jessica Fernandez, age 10

Fitzgerald Fuentes, age 13

been entertaining guests for years. The trainers are pursuing a new dream; soon, guests will be able to swim with the dolphins.

The bus returns to Kapiolani Park, a onetime royal racecourse set between the ocean, Diamond Head, and Waikiki. Our families have worked hard for this respite in the park. They have entered and scaled an ancient volcano. They have gazed beyond a lighthouse to a sea filled with

Julia Chun, grandmother, age 65

LIKE THE WAVES, GOD IS STRONG. HE CAN KNOCK DOWN ANYTHING THAT
IS IN HIS WAY. THE WAVES SHOW GOD'S STRENGTH.

Fitzgerald Fuentes, age 13

souls, souls seeking something beyond the safety of the shore. They excitedly recall cheering and encouraging three playful dolphins as they leaped from home to heaven to home again.

Now it's time to rest and enjoy a hearty lunch and drink in all the sights across the acres of glorious green grass. Families flying kites, barbecuing in the ironwood groves, jogging, watching team games, taking in the weekend exhibits, and swimming at the nearby Kama'aina ("Local") Beach. There is the Honolulu Zoo as well as a lovely aquarium. But most hearts come simply to play and people watch.

Janinne Jurin

Jessica Fernandez, age 10

THE TWO GRANDPARENTS WHO ARE
WITH US, THEY ARE SO HAPPY AND
TELLING EVERYBODY THIS IS REALLY
WONDERFUL. FOR GOD HAS PUT US
TOGETHER, EVEN CONSIDERING HOW
BUSY WE ARE... JUST TO SEE HIM.

Lourdes Cabinatan, mother, age 52

The children and their families seek God in these popular family spots, and not surprisingly, they find God in one another. They climb and gaze in wonder at the beauty of the world, but when they look into each other's eyes they find God gazing back. One child finds God in the generosity of an older gentleman sharing his treasure and time on the climb up Diamond Head. A daughter and mother find God in each other. A little boy finds God in himself. One young heart says it best when she likens people to "God's lovely dreams for the future."

Chapter 6

"I See God Waiting for Someone to Talk To"

Carlynn Caraang, age 13

Michelle Taylor, mother, age 32

Arthur Aiwohi V, age 6

Bronson Taylor, age 67

I SEE GOD IN THE HAWAIIAN FLAG. WHATEVER WE ARE, RACE OR COLOR, WE WILL STILL STAND AS ONE.

Lamborie Aiwohi, mother, age 33

THE CHILDREN AND THEIR FAMILIES ABOARD BUS SIX HEAD STRAIGHT FOR DOWNTOWN HONOLULU. THEY WILL SEEK GOD IN THE HEART OF HAWAII'S STATE GOVERNMENT. THEIR FIRST STOP IS THE CAPITOL, AN ARCHITECTURAL WONDER WITH ITS VOLCANO-SHAPED ROOF OPEN TO THE SKY. MANY OF OUR FAMILIES HAVE NEVER DREAMED THEY WOULD TOUR THE OFFICES OF HAWAII'S STATE LEADERS. HERE THEY VISIT THE OFFICES OF BOTH GOVERNOR BENJAMIN CAYETANO AND SENATOR BRIAN KANNO FROM EWA BEACH.

A great honor awaits them when they enter the legislative chambers. State Representative Paul Oshiro, also from Ewa Beach, leads the legislative body in recognizing the students and families of Our Lady of Perpetual Help School. "These children and their families are writing a book today. However, I ask my colleagues to bow your heads in prayer, because more important, these families are seeking God. And I pray that they find Him here." So members of the legislature solemnly bow their heads and pray for the success of this endeavor. The children and their families are dazzled.

I SAW GOD
ON TOP
OF THE
BUILDING.

Jasper Alino, age 5

Jasper Alino

I FEEL GOD
PROTECTING
AND WATCH-
ING OVER THE
GOVERNOR.

Rodrigo Hilario, age 10

THE SUPREME COURT
IS WHERE I SEE GOD.
THEY ARE A SECOND
CHANCE FOR PEOPLE
AND GOD ENDLESSLY
FORGIVES.

Brian Hinkle, age 13

Lamborie Aiwohi

Arthur Aiwohi V

I TOOK A PICTURE OF GOD IN THE FORM OF A KING.

Arthur Aiwohi V, age 6

The families walk to the King Kamehameha statue in front of the State Judiciary Building. On the way they pass the Iolani Palace that King David Kalakaua constructed in 1882. His sister, Queen Liliu'okalani, was later imprisoned here and was shamefully forced to abdicate the throne in 1893. The families pause at the gates and think upon a land that was once ruled by the "Merry Monarch."

They cross the street and stand in front of King Kamehameha. This statue is a replica of another

GOD IS LIFE, PURITY, AND LOVE WHICH WE SEE EVERY DAY IN OUR CHILDREN.

Araceli Hurley, teacher, age 28

Christina Akins, age 22

I SEE GOD LYING ON THE GROUND AND THINKING OF THE CREATION HE HAS MADE.

Carlynn Caraang, age 13

Pearl Taylor, grandmother, age 60

cast in Italy and lost in a shipwreck around Cape Horn. The original was salvaged and now stands proudly on the Big Island. On state holidays the statue is festooned with gigantic exotic flower leis befitting the king who first united the islands of Hawaii. Directly behind him is the State Judiciary Building with its lovely clock tower. The families tour this building, home of the Supreme Court. Many hearts see God in the light spilling through the stained-glass ceiling onto the marble floor.

Carlynn Caraang, age 13

THIS IS A PICTURE
ABOUT A GRAVE
THAT IS A FAMILY
MEMBER.
HE DIED WHEN I WAS
TWO YEARS OLD.
I SEE GOD, BECAUSE
MY DAD WAS BURIED
THERE. GOD IS
PROTECTING HIM.

Rodrigo Hilario, age 10

Kawaiahao Church is the last place our families visit. Blocks cut from coral and timber were used to build this church, the site of royal coronations. Today the families arrive just in time to witness a wedding. The families reverently enter the church, then proceed to a tiny cemetery tucked protectively behind it. They reflect upon lives that walked the earth long ago. Ten-year-old Rodrigo Hilario takes a picture of a grave. He remembers his father, who died when he was only two years old. Rodrigo writes simply, "I see God because my dad was buried there. God is protecting him."

They cross King Street back to the Iolani Palace grounds to enjoy a picnic lunch before boarding their bus for the ride back to school. One dazzling day spent in downtown Honolulu fills

Lamborie Aiwohi, mother, age 33

Rachel Taylor

I SEE GOD
IN HAPPINESS.

Raquel Taylor, age 8

I SEE GOD IN THE MANY COLORS.

Raquel Taylor

their spirits with memories. Although there is strict separation of church and state, and sometimes God appears to be waiting for someone to talk to, the children and their families find God here. God is in the prayers offered in the rotunda of the state legislature. God is seen in the crosses embedded on the walls of the Iolani Palace. They find God in the form of a king and in second chances meted out by the supreme court. God is seen in a wedding party hurrying to church. And God is present in a tiny cemetery behind the church.

Yes, God may be waiting for someone to talk to, but He doesn't have to wait long—not on this day.

Chapter 7

"I See God Playing Hide-and-Go-Seek"

Tiffany Peters, age 12

Andrea Moore, age 9

Cheryl Ho, mother, age 34

I SEE GOD IN THE SKY
BECAUSE THAT IS WHERE HE REIGNS,
WHERE HE LIVES, WHERE HE WATCHES OVER US.

Tiffany Peters, age 12

THERE MOM...OVERTHERE...IN THE CLOUD...THERE...I SEE HIM!

Bradley Akana, age 5

Shanita Akana, mother, age 33

THE FAMILIES RIDING BUS SEVEN PLAY A GAME OF HIDE-AND-GO-SEEK WITH GOD, AND GOD IS PLAYFUL TODAY. KAREN PETERSON, A JOURNALIST ASSIGNED BY THE HONOLULU ADVERTISER TO COVER THE EVENT, DECIDES TO FOLLOW ONE CHILD'S JOURNEY IN SEARCH OF GOD. IN FACT, THE MOMENT LEAH JOY SARVIDA STEPS OFF THE BUS AT KEAIWA HEIAU STATE RECREATION AREA, THEIR FIRST STOP, KAREN BEGINS TO TIME LEAH. How long will it take one eight-year-old child to find God? Other children and family members raise their cameras almost immediately. But not Leah Joy. God has found a good hiding place. Suddenly, Leah sees God. She raises her camera to the tree branches high above and snaps His picture. Karen looks at her watch. It has taken Leah Joy exactly fourteen minutes. When asked by the journalist if Leah had ever seen God before, she whispers back, "No, this is my first time."

Philip Gapusan

I SEE GOD IN THE
BUSHES BECAUSE I
THINK HE IS HIDING
FROM ME.

Philip Gapusan, age 7

Leah Joy Sarvida

I SAW GOD IN A
TREE BECAUSE I
KNOW HE WATCHES
OVER THIS TREE.

Leah Joy Sarvida, age 8

Andrea Moore, age 9

I SEE GOD IN ME
BECAUSE I AM A
NICE AND CARING
PERSON.

Leah Joy Sarvida

Denal Jenkins

GOD LIVES IN THE FOREST.

Brock Akana, age 7

John Akana, father, age 31

Bryson Ho, age 13

I TOOK A PICTURE OF A BUSH BECAUSE GOD IS HIDING IN IT.

Kyle Akana, age 10

I FOUND GOD IN THE TREES.
GOD IS LIVING IN THEM. THESE TREES ARE SO GRACIOUS.

Denal Jenkins, age 13

This is not the typical news item that would interest a daily newspaper. Yet Karen Peterson and photographer Deborah Booker were determined to cover this event. To get here this April morning required some ingenuity on their part. In the morning budget meeting, Deborah insisted, "I want to cover that little school from Ewa Beach that is seeking 'beauty in the gathering place.'"

"Beauty?" said the editor.

"Yes. Beauty," answered the photographer.

When they left the meeting, Karen asked Deborah, "Why did you say beauty? They're looking for God."

"Karen, do you really believe they would let us cover this if they knew it was God?"

"You're right. Let's go"

I SEE GOD IN THE FISH
BECAUSE FISH ARE GOD'S GIFT TO US CHILDREN.

Sherri-Ann Carganilla, age 8

Malory Ahlo, age 11

Our families' journey takes them to the Aiea Loop trail, where they hike up the Koolau Mountain Range overlooking Pearl Harbor and the great central plain of Oahu and across to the parallel Waianae Range. The hike takes them under a canopy of eucalyptus trees and on to a broad trail flanked by lacy ironwood and soaring Norfolk pines. When our weary hikers descend, they take a short ride to the Moanalua Gardens. Here they enjoy a lovely grassy park shaded by majestically spreading monkeypod trees. King Kamehameha V's summer cottage sits here at the foot of a taro pond. The children also enjoy ponds with lilies and fat carp of many colors.

After this restful stay, the families journey to the Honolulu International Airport to drop off a few passengers. A priest, a science teacher, and a mother board a Bell 206 Jet Ranger helicopter to seek God from the skies of Oahu. Pilot Doug O'Sullivan takes his passengers on a circle island tour thanks to the generosity of Richard Schuman, owner of Makani Kai Helicopters.

I FOUND GOD EVERYWHERE I WENT!
FROM WAY UP IN THE SKY TO THE GROUND. THERE IS NO LIMIT
BECAUSE GOD IS EVERYWHERE, ESPECIALLY IN PEOPLE'S HEARTS.

Denal Jenkins, age 13

Bradley Ho, age 8

Shanita Akana

Shanita Akana, mother, age 33

Father Robert Phelps, pastor, age 57

FORD ISLAND BRIDGE, PEARL HARBOR, AND THE ARIZONA MEMORIAL. GOD IS PRESENT IN HIS REBUILDING OF AN AREA THAT WAS SEVERELY DAMAGED FIFTY YEARS AGO BY THE WAR.

Cesar Carganilla, father, age 32

Tiffany Peters

I SEE GOD PLAYING HIDE AND GO SEEK WHILE THE GENTLE RAIN DRIZZLES DOWN.

Tiffany Peters, age 12

After they bid aloha to the excited passengers, the families enjoy lunch by the protected waters of Keehi Lagoon, parallel to the airport's runway. Yvonne Ahlo, a grandmother, notes the heavy disappointment in the children who had longed to fly. She calls everyone together and says simply: "The passengers need our help. I want you to sit quietly and imagine yourself up in that big helicopter. If you were flying right now, where would you find God? Let's all ride that helicopter in spirit and write where we find God."

Shanita Akana, mother, age 33

I SEE GOD IN THE GATHERING PLACE.

Andrea Moore

John Akana, father, age 31

CHILDREN. I SEE GOD IN CHILDREN.

Andrea Moore, age 9

Surely God was guiding this grandmother. In reality, the passengers aboard the helicopter needed the families down below. The priest, the science teacher, and the mother were so filled with awe that they forgot to write. The three of them took many photos from the air, but wrote nothing in their notebooks. But thanks to the lovely imaginings of the families on the beach, God filled in the gaps.

Later that day, Karen Peterson submitted her article to the same editor. She stamped her foot: "It was God they were seeking, and I found Him too!"

And so God was featured in Section A of the *Advertiser*'s Sunday edition.

Chapter 8

"Another of God's Creatures Has the Chance to Claim the Sky"

Judyline Corpuz, age 14

Brian Baldovino, age 8

Marco Corpuz, age 10

Gino Aguilar, age 10

B US EIGHT PROCEEDS TOWN-BOUND ON H-1, ON A JOURNEY THROUGH HAWAII'S UNIQUE MODERN HISTORY. THE DRIVER TAKES THE PEARL HARBOR EXIT AND ARRIVES AT THE GREAT NAVAL BASE. THE GATE IS GUARDED BY STERN MARINE SENTRIES, BUT A SMILING JERRI MOORE, U.S. PACIFIC PUBLIC AFFAIRS SPECIALIST, IS WAITING TO GREET THESE VIP GUESTS. SHE BOARDS AND DIRECTS THE BUS DRIVER TO A PARKING LOT NEAR THE USS *PAUL HAMILTON DDG 60*. The children and their families will seek God on a U.S. Navy destroyer. GSM2 Newton, EM2 Figuero, and EN1 Jackson serve as tour guides through the ship. The children especially enjoy the pilothouse on the bridge, where they take turns spinning in the captain's chair, trying his job on for size.

I SAW GOD IN A FLAG BECAUSE IT MEANS WE FOUGHT FOR OUR FREE-DOM AND GOD HELPED US TO DO THAT.

Michael Sarmiento, age 9

THE MAST SEEMS TO BE LIFTING ITS ARMS AS IF TO ASK A BLESSING ON THE SHIP.

Susan Maxey, mother, age 35

Anne Jasper, mother, age 32

Gino Aguilar

I SEE GOD IN THIS PICTURE BECAUSE WHEN I LOOK AT THIS CONSOLE, I IMAGINE THAT GOD WOULD SIT AT A CONSOLE LIKE THIS AND CONTROL THE EARTH. FOR EXAMPLE, HE WOULD TELL THE SUN WHEN TO COME UP AND WHERE THE WINDS SHOULD BLOW AND WHERE IT WILL RAIN.

Justin Kessler, age 13

THERE HE IS! GOD IS IN THAT FLYING BOX! IT LOOKS AS IF HE IS WATCHING EVERYONE IN SIGHT. IT LOOKS AS IF HE IS TRYING TO TELL US SOMETHING.

Doria Maxey, age 12

Jovenard Mapanao, age 7

I TOOK A PICTURE OF A TOWER BECAUSE IT IS OLD AND GOD HELD IT TOGETHER.

Michael Sarmiento, age 9

Rochelle Sarmiento, mother, age 33

Next, Bus Eight crosses over the Admiral Bernard "Chick" Clarey Bridge, which has been open only eight days. The striking span, almost a mile long, links the busy naval base with Ford Island, home to "Battleship Row," attacked by the Japanese on the morning of December 7, 1941. Its signature USS Arizona Memorial is soon to be joined by the renowned USS *Missouri*, scene of the formal Japanese surrender in Tokyo Bay in 1945. The families tour by bus the 450 acres of Ford Island as Chief Warrant Officer Keck, their escort, shares stories of an era just closing.

Judyline Corpuz

Susan Maxey, mother, age 39

SUNNY HAWAIIAN SKY. "HELLO GOD, HOW ARE YOU TODAY?"
Judyline Corpuz, age 14

Peter Gascon

THE WAVING SUGAR CANE, SO SWEET, JUST LIKE GOD'S LOVE FOR US IS SWEET.

Peter Gascon, father, age 41

The bus goes back across the bridge and heads for the freeway and their next stop, the Waipahu Cultural Garden Park, where they rest and lunch at picnic tables surrounded by flowers and shady trees. Then the families pass through a tunnel and travel back in time to when the sugarcane and pineapple plantation owners ruled territorial Hawaii. Plantation Village serves as a monument to the immigrants who came to work the cane fields as children from as far away as the Philippines, Korea, Japan, China, Puerto Rico, and Portugal. Some of our families are their descendants. They are

IN THE DARKNESS THERE IS HOPE

A BIRD'S EGGSHELL.
GOD HAS ONCE AGAIN
GIVEN LIFE. ANOTHER OF
GOD'S CREATURES HAS
THE CHANCE TO CLAIM
THE SKY.

Judyline Corpuz, age 14

Judyline Corpuz

I SEE GOD IN THIS PICTURE
BECAUSE YOU CAN'T REAL-
LY SEE GOD AND YOU
DON'T ALWAYS KNOW WHAT
HE WANTS YOU TO DO, YOU
JUST KNOW HE IS THERE.

Justin Kessler, age 13

awed by the faith of those brave souls. Every home had a prayer corner. Our families walk through a plantation store, visit Filipino camp dwellings, and enjoy the serenity of the Japanese and Chinese temples. Soon it is time to make the short journey back to school.

One child finds a miraculous symbol of hope for this day's images of a dramatic and sometimes harsh history and the possibilities for renewed life. Fourteen-year-old Judyline Corpuz notices a fragile egg lying in the grass and comments on the hope—"Another one of God's creatures has the chance to claim the sky." Yes, they all were given that God-driven potential, whether they walk the steel decks of a U.S. naval destroyer or dream of bridging two communities or labored long ago in the red dirt growing the cane. Life is as fragile as the eggshell yet promises the glory of the sky.

Left: Judith Booth, teacher, age 52

Susan Maxey, mother, age 35

Chapter 9

"It's You I See!"

Peggy Crowell, grandmother, age 60

Thomas Suster, father, age 44

131

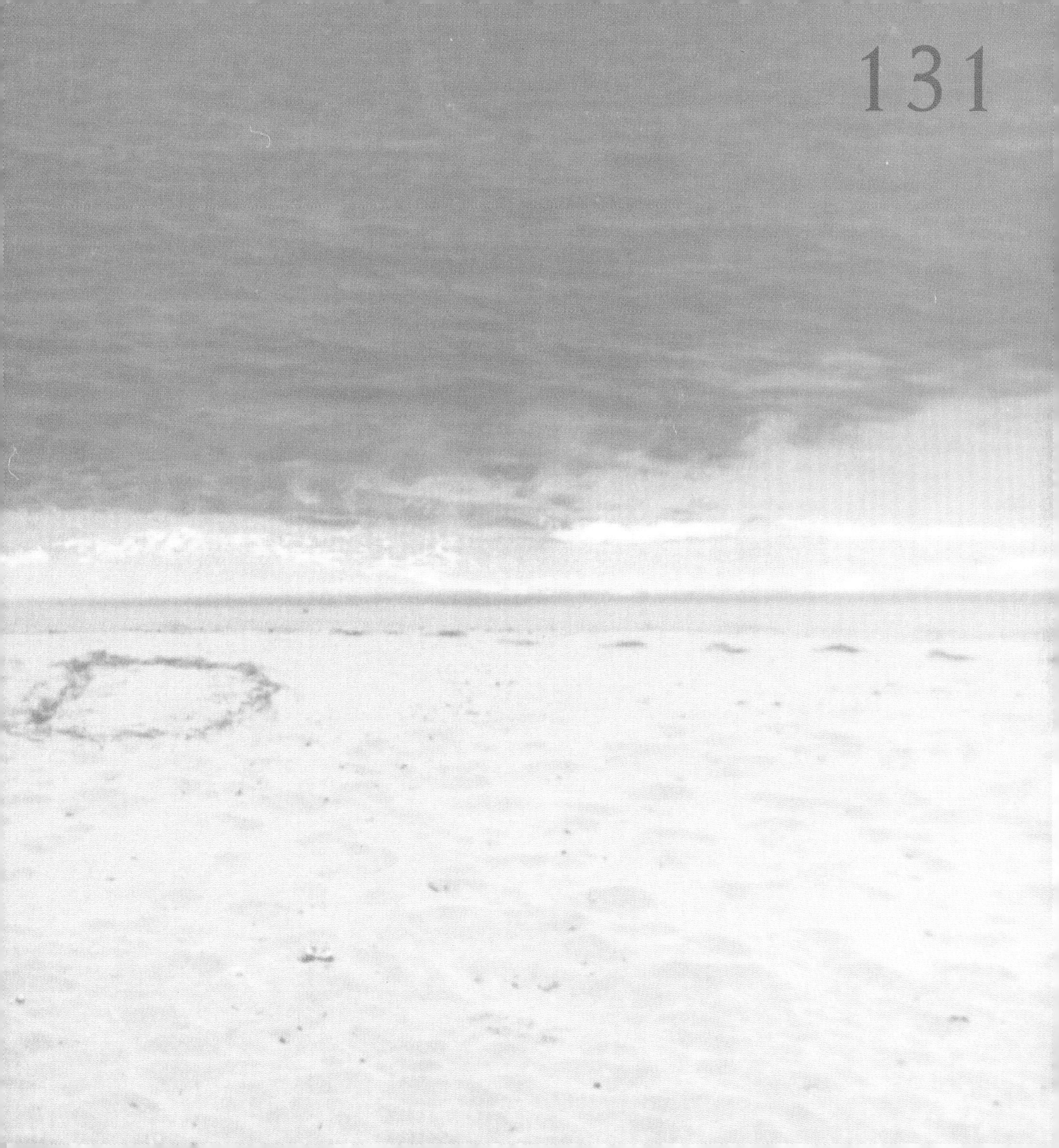

Nani Kumia

ONLY YOU GOD CAN CREATE SUCH BEAUTY. A PLACE FOR BIRDS TO REST.
A PLACE FOR ME TO REST.

Nani Kumia, grandmother, age 62

Bus Nine is singularly blessed by the presence of three grandmothers, dear friends whose interactions with the mothers, fathers, and children leave a profound impression on the families' search for God. Virgie Chong, Nani Kumia, and Peggy Crowell have been gathering in each other's homes to pray together since 1978. During this journey, a mother opens her heart to them and feels a healing peace; they become family for the day. She takes a photo that captures their inner light.

At the Wahiawa Botanic Gardens our families walk in beauty, twenty-seven acres of beauty. Flowers, trees, and spice plants from around the world dazzle the senses. Many birds call this oasis home and give a concert on the wing as they sing throughout the oasis. The families stroll, admire the lush natural beauty, and rest peacefully on benches, enjoying one another until it's time to board the bus for the next secret destination.

I SEE GOD
IN THIS GIANT TREE.

Brandon Rafanan, age 5

Brandon Rafanan

ARE THESE THE
STAIRS THAT MY PAPA
FAUROT AND PAPA
TIQUI TOOK TO HEAVEN
TO SEE GOD? GOD,
ARE MY PAPA'S OKAY?

Blaize Faurot, age 5

Blaize Faurot

CAN YOU SEE GOD? I DID. I CAN'T BELIEVE I DID.
SEE HIM? HE'S THE SUN OF OUR MORNING.
HE MAKES MY LIFE FULL OF LIFE.
HE SHINES UPON US.
OUR GOD, OUR LIGHT, OUR LOVE.

Krystle Rafanan, age 13

Krystle Rafanan

I SEE GOD IN MY MOM'S HANDS BECAUSE SHE ALWAYS WORKS HARD AND WHEN SHE WORKS HARD, SHE USES HER BEAUTIFUL HANDS.

Melissa Rabanal, age 12

Tavon Spiller, age 9

PINEAPPLE: I SAW GOD IN HIS GIFT OF LIFE AND HIS SWEETNESS.

Thomas Suster, father, age 44

Melissa Rabanal

They drive on Kamehameha Highway through miles of vast pineapple fields. The driver stops at the Dole Pineapple Pavilion, where the families buy souvenirs and treat all the children to pineapple snacks and ice cream treats as they would on any family outing. They walk in a pineapple field, admiring the sweet harvest from the red earth.

Their next stop will take them briefly through Schofield Barracks, with the majestic Waianae Range close by, perhaps the most beautiful military base in the world. Yet it is the thoughtfulness of soldiers in an army truck that captivates the attention of the youngest of the seekers. The soldiers pause in their work to play "army" with the children. Just outside the base's main Macomb Gate, the

Thomas Suster, father, age 44

I SEE GOD IN ME!

Gregory Suster, age 7

Gregory Suster

I SEE GOD IN
DOLE FOOD.

Robert Suster, age 7

Melissa Rabanal, age 12

GOD WAS TAKING THE DIRT TO WHERE EVERYONE WAS WORKING.

Blaize Faurot, age 5

Thomas Suster, father, age 44

GOD IS OUR CENTER OF ATTENTION
AND WE SURROUND HIM LIKE TREES AROUND THIS ISLAND.

Ian Kim, age 13

bus arrives at Lake Wilson, the largest body of fresh water on Oahu. There is a little island named Woodwinds. Fishermen come to find peace casting their lines into the glassy lake, green because the water is rich in algae.

Their final destination is Mokuleia Beach Park, on the rural North Shore. Weekdays this park is all but deserted. The children stare at the magical gliders from the nearby Dillingham Airfield floating silently in the updraft caused by the steep Waianae Range nearby. Brilliant crests of surf break across the outer reef before surging rhythmically to the shorebreak. The families spend time playing on the beach, which they have to themselves. One father writes a message in giant letters in the

Rommel Halili, age 11

I FOUND GOD IN THIS MAN.
HE WAS FULL OF ALOHA. HE WAS ENJOYING
THE COOL BREEZE AND HIS SPAM, RICE, AND
VEGETABLES. HE LOOKED LIKE HE ONLY
WANTED SOME TIME WITH GOD.

Krystle Rafanan, age 13

Peggy Crowell, age 60   Ian Kim, age 13   Thomas Suster, age 44   Peggy Crowell, age 60

heavy golden sand. After a leisurely lunch and one more stroll along the shore, the families return to the bus for the hour-long ride home, southward across the great central plain.

Throughout the day the children and their families express astonishment that they can indeed see God. They turn to each other in wonder. One child excitedly exclaims, "Can you see God? I can't believe I did. See Him?" The grace of the grandmothers is that they see God and do not turn away in wonder. They gaze long into the face of God and speak their hearts to Him. One grandmother states simply, "It's You I see." These grandmothers are not shy to speak to God. They've already met. And they are friends.

Chapter 10

"God Spreads His Love to All of Us"

Maggie Liuzzi, age 13

George Toro, grandfather, age 77

Earl Recitis, age 9

Trish Liuzzi

GOD GATHERS AMONG THE OLD
AND NEW IN HALEIWA TOWN.

Trish Liuzzi, mother, age 49

Juanita Colon, grandmother, age 64

T HE CHILDREN AND THEIR FAMILIES JOYFULLY BOARD BUS TEN AND HEAD FOR THE NORTH
SHORE. IT IS A BEAUTIFUL DRIVE THROUGH THE LEILEHUA PLATEAU, LAND OF PINEAPPLE
AND CANE FIELDS. THIS GREEN SADDLE LIES BETWEEN TWO CLOUD-COVERED MOUNTAIN
RANGES—THE WAIANAE MOUNTAINS TO THE WEST AND THE KOOLAU MOUNTAINS TO THE EAST.
HAWAIIAN LEGEND INSISTS THAT THIS IS THE BIRTHPLACE OF ALL RAINBOWS.

One little girl simply cannot sit still during the ride. Her antsy demeanor becomes apparent
to all the passengers on the bus. Finally, one mother asks the little girl, "Are you excited?"

"Yes!" she exclaims. "I am going to see God today." Laughter rolls through the bus.

Their first stop is the beach town of Haleiwa, gateway to the North Shore and the surfing cap-
ital of the world. Surfers from all over the world flock to these beaches to challenge the surging walls
of water. With its low clapboard false-fronted buildings, Haleiwa looks like an old western town. The
families explore the boutiques and galleries and specialty stores that cater to every ocean sport.

I SEE THIS LEAF
AS GOD'S HAND.
WHEN IT RAINS, IT
CATCHES THE
RAINDROPS. AND
WHEN WE CRY, HIS
HAND CATCHES
OUR TEARS.

Larma Torres, sister, age 20

Vivian Toro, grandmother, age 70

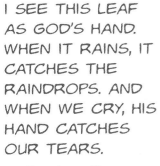

Perla Recitis, mother, age 38

Jennifer Colon, mother, age 30

WITH HIS
UNDYING LOVE,
GOD MADE THIS.

Maggie Liuzzi, age 13

Evangeline Nartatez

Jaime Sacayanan, age 12

GOD GIVES US THESE THINGS TO HELP US ENJOY THE WATERS HE CREATED.

Anne Rabacal, age 7

Anne Rabacal

OLD TORN HOUSE. I BELIEVE THIS IS AN ACT OF GOD, THEREFORE GOD IS HERE.

Evangeline Nartatez, age 5

They drive on to the lush Waimea Valley. They play with peacocks on the roadside. They walk deep into a banana grove. They chance upon an old abandoned plantation home overgrown with foliage. The driver then ushers them back down to their next stop—Waimea Bay, with its spectacular expanse of beach, home to the monstrous thirty-foot winter waves. On this April morning the surf is quiet. By summer the awesome North Shore waves will be nearly flat.

Our families drive to Pupukea Beach Park and Sharks Cove. Despite the name, sharks do not

Rommel Halili, age 11

I SEE GOD IN A WINDSURFER.

Gregory Suster, age 7

Jaime Sacayanan, age 12

Anne Rabacal

Trish Liuzzi, mother, age 49

I SEE GOD IN THE VAN BECAUSE HE IS WAVING AT ME, ENJOYING HIS GOOD TIME.

Daniel Colon, age 11

YOU CAN SEE THE GENTLENESS OF GOD. THEN YOU SEE THE POWER.

Maggie Liuzzi, age 13

frequent these waters. The cove is rich with marine life and is a prime location for divers and snorkelers. Our families explore a playground of tide pools that line the rocky shore, paying special care because these rocks are razor sharp.

Our beachcombers move on to Sunset Beach, another favorite with killer waves to challenge the experienced surfer. Yet come summertime, this beach invites families to come and play in the sticky golden sand, building castles and frolicking in the gentle shorebreak.

Earl Recitis, age 9

Ignacio Nartatez, father, age 32

I SEE GOD IN THE MOUNTAIN'S HEART. Kylee Rabacal, age 7

IN EVERY SACRED HEIAU YOU'LL FIND GOD.

George Toro, grandfather, age 77

Kylee Rabacal

The driver now turns in from the ocean, carefully negotiating hairpin turns up the Pupukea bluff, and then encounters speed bumps along a narrow road until he arrives at the day's final destination—Pu'u O Mahuka Heiau State Monument. This *heiau*, or temple, is a sacred place of worship and burial ground for members of the Hawaiian royal family that is thought to be at least five hundred years old. This is the largest *heiau* on the island open to the general public. Every rock and plant and even the dirt is considered sacred and must not be disturbed—not even a pebble may be taken. Pu'u O Mahuka means "Hill of Escape" in Hawaiian. The families prayerfully walk around the great oblong structure of loose lava rock and sense the *mana*, the heavy spirituality, here. The offerings of fruit brought by the Hawaiians and so carefully placed remind the children of an altar in a church. The children and

I SEE GOD IN THE PLANT AREA BECAUSE HE PLANTED US LIKE TREES.

Daniel Colon, age 11

Perla Recitis, mother, age 38

GOD REMINDS ME TO HANG ON WHEN THE GOING GETS TOUGH.

Jennifer Colon, mother, age 30

Juanita Colon, grandmother, age 64

Jennifer Colon

their families gaze in awe at the sweeping panoramic view of the North Shore to distant windswept Kaena Point. They are reluctant to leave this sacred place to make their journey home.

Yet God spreads His love beyond this day. Trish Liuzzi, a mother who spent the day with her daughter in search of God, carries His love to work. Trish is a hospice nurse. Her primary duty is to peacefully prepare her patients and their families for the final journey home to God. She is able to comfort and console the families and their loved ones nearing death with her unwavering conviction that there is a God, a loving God. She knows this for a fact. She met God one April morning on a journey to the North Shore of Oahu. Further, she insists, "I wasn't the only one. All the families on my bus found God."

Chapter 11

"I Felt God's Presence All Around Me"

Shane Ahlo, age 9

Precious Gonzales, age 19

Glenn de Laura, father, age 42

Ingrid Angela Salazar, age 7

I FOUND GOD IN THE BEAUTIFUL FLOWERS WITH RED PETALS. THEY REMIND ME OF GOD'S FLAMING LOVE FOR US ALL.

Maria Salazar, mother, age 34

EXCITEMENT MOUNTS ON BUS ELEVEN AS THE DRIVER GOES "DIAMOND HEAD" (I.E., EASTWARD) ON H-1 TO THE PALI EXIT DOWNTOWN. ONE FATHER FINDS GOD IN A CHILD SITTING BESIDE HIM. SCOTT MUNSON TAKES SEVERAL PHOTOS OF HIS SON, THOMAS, AND WRITES: "I SEE GOD WHEN I SEE MY SON SMILING AND I KNOW HE IS HAPPY." THE DRIVE UP NU'UANU VALLEY IS SPECTACULAR; HAWAIIAN ROYALTY FAVORED NU'UANU FOR THEIR HOMES.

The misty green velvet of the jungle-clad Koolau Mountain Range casts a morning shadow down the lush valley. They pass through the dark Pali tunnel and emerge to a breathtaking vista of the verdant windward shore communities below and the vast blue ocean beyond. A hairpin turn down through wild banana groves brings them to the St. Stephen's Diocesan Center for an

I SEE GOD AT ST. STEPHEN'S DIOCESAN CENTER BECAUSE THIS IS WHERE PEOPLE LIVE PEACEFULLY.

Thomas Munson, age 11

Shane Ahlo

AS I KNELT DOWN IN FRONT OF MOTHER MARY, I FELT GOD'S PRESENCE ALL AROUND ME.

Shane Ahlo, age 9

Shane Ahlo

Scott Munson

I SEE GOD IN THE TRANQUILLITY AND CLEANLINESS OF ST. STEPHEN'S.

Scott Munson, father, age 47

unannounced visit. Here the families freely wander the fifteen-acre property nestled in the slope of Pu'u Konahuanui, the highest peak of the Koolaus. St. Stephen's once was plantation owner Harold K. L. Castle's mansion. The estate then became a seminary and is now home to the Roman Catholic bishop, church offices, a convent for Carmelite nuns, and a retreat center. A prayerful peacefulness surrounds the families as they walk the land graced with tropical foliage, flowers, and religious grotto's.

TWO YELLOW
ANGEL FISH
SWIMMING
AROUND.
IF THESE ARE
ANGELS, GOD
MUST BE NEAR.

Joshua de Laura, age 14

Jesus Schellhorn, age 6

Glenn de Laura, father, age 42

I SEE GOD IN THE RED AND THE BLUE FISH
BECAUSE THEY ARE FAST AND CUNNING.

Thomas Munson, age 11

Ingrid Angela Salazar

Our families board the bus and continue down to Kaneohe Bay, Hawaii's largest, spectacularly framed by the Koolau Range. The cooling northwesterly trade winds chase a constant train of clouds across the Pacific, banking them up against the three-thousand-foot *pali* ("barrier") and releasing the rainwater that has sculpted an awesome scalloped curtain of fluted cliffs. At Heeia Pier they board the *Coral Queen*, a forty-eight-foot glass-bottom boat. Sig Schuster, president and owner of Kaneohe Bay Cruises, generously donated the use of this vessel for a two-hour tour of the beautiful shallow waters. The children and their families stare in wonder through the transparent water at the secret world in the coral reefs. The colorful Achilles tang, the bullethead parrotfish, and the renowned Potter's angelfish enchant the children and their families. When the *Coral Queen* returns to the pier the children are reluctant to leave. They linger onboard until their mothers and fathers finally take their hands and lead them across the brow.

I SAW GOD ON THE BOTTOM OF THE OCEAN BECAUSE IT'S SO BEAUTIFUL DOWN THERE AND VERY CLEAN. THE CORALS ARE SO PERFECT THE WAY THEY GROW. I THINK THAT'S THE BEST PLACE TO STAY.

Rommel Raymundo, age 5

Rommel Raymundo

Ingrid Angela Salazar

I SEE GOD IN PAPAYAS BECAUSE THEY ARE GOOD- JUST LIKE HIM

Adam Vorlicky, age 14

I FOUND GOD IN THE BIRDS BECAUSE THEY ARE BEAUTIFUL AS ANGELS.

Ingrid Angela Salazar, age 7

The last stop is for lunch at Kaneohe Bay Beach Park, sheltered by the volcanoes of the Mokapu Peninsula across the water. The mothers and fathers rest at picnic tables, quietly talking while the children run free in the grass, burning up the excess energy stored up during their sedentary morning. Soon they must board the bus for the long trip home.

God drew very near this group today. From the moment the bus left the school parking lot, the children and their families sensed His presence. A father mused that God must have taken the day off to be with them on this journey. A little boy fell to his knees at the foot of a religious statue and later explained, "I felt God's presence all around me." God was felt in the wind, the waters, the quiet, and in the sudden appearance of angelfish. A fourteen-year-old boy wisely observed, "If these are angels, God must be near."

Chapter 12

"I See God's Heart"

Royce Guerra, age 13

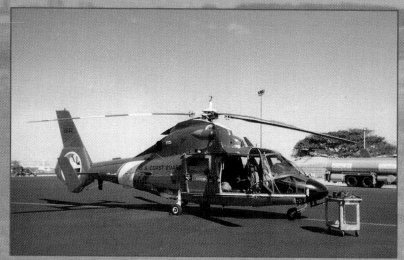

David Moore, father, age 38

Shirley Castro, mother, age 54

Andrew Agustin

Shirley Castro, mother, age 54

I SAW HIM IN
THIS TRAIN THAT
HELPED PEOPLE
TRAVEL FROM
ONE PLACE TO
ANOTHER LONG
AGO.

Lisa Maghamil, mother, age 33

Andrew Agustin

THE FAMILIES ABOARD BUS TWELVE SEEK GOD IN THEIR OWN BACK-YARD. THEIR FIRST DESTINATION TAKES THEM THROUGH THE HAND-SOME PLANTATION TOWN OF EWA, WITH ITS QUIET HOMES AND WESTERN-STYLE WOODEN BUILDINGS SHADED BY ENORMOUS BANYAN TREES. Beyond the abandoned sugar mill they are greeted by crowing roosters and tiny wooden plantation-style cabins still used for homes. The bus stops at the Hawaiian Railway Society's train yard. The families board Train 302, powered by a diesel electric locomotive, and roll six and a half miles west along the old Oahu Railway and Land Company right-of-way, a ninety-minute journey. This corner of the island has a rich history, especially pertaining to the sugar plantation era.

Bus Twelve then goes back through the town as they head toward Barber's Point Naval Air Station. Passing marine sentries, they follow the road along the ocean until it dead-ends at the entrance to the Coast Guard Air Station. Our children and their families will be the VIP guests of Captain Roger Whorton, commanding officer of the facility.

They are treated to a mock helicopter hoist demonstration used in a search-and-rescue operation. Then the children have the chance of a lifetime; they get to sit in the pilot's seat of an HH65-A Dolphin, a maritime search-and-rescue helicopter. The Coast Guard maintains four of these at this facility.

Rose Delizo, age 10

James Vahlsing, grandfather, age 56

Lorra Naholowa'a

I FOUND GOD IN THE RESCUE HELICOPTER WHICH HELPS THE RESCUERS TO RESCUE THOSE IN NEED MUCH FASTER THAN ON FOOT.

Janeen Pasion, age 13

I SEE GOD IN A PLANE AND A HELI-COPTER BECAUSE THEY FLY.

Andrew Agustin, age 6

BIGGER THAN LIFE, SMALLER THAN GOD.

Lorra Naholowa'a, auntie, age 32

Next they tour the workhorse of the Coast Guard—*Hercules*, an HC130 multimission aircraft. *Hercules* carries a crew of seven and can go just about anywhere and do just about anything. It has flown three hundred miles offshore to drop a life raft; it has dropped Cub Scout books to Kwajalein, in the Marshall Islands. This aircraft is used for most of the search-and-rescue operations here in Hawaii. Whatever the need, the Coast Guard is ready to help. They have rescued divers in trouble, hikers trapped on cliffs, and hapless sailors aboard burning and sinking vessels of all sizes.

Our families are ready for a rest at the nearby Ewa Beach Park. Given its proximity to two military installations and housing, this park is a favorite of military and local families. Weekends, they come to enjoy a lazy afternoon picnic, looking out across the gentle waves at Diamond Head and Waikiki.

Sheryl Agustin, age 9   Lorra Naholowa'a, auntie, age 32

I SEE GOD'S HEART.

Royce Guerra, age 13

Lorra Naholowa'a

It is a lovely spot to enjoy the sunrise. The children notice the Waikiki Health Center's Care Van parked here to give medical attention to the homeless. The children walk past an altar of white stones, a reminder of a life once lived. After lunch, the children walk the broad straight beach and play in the sand before they board the bus for school, only minutes away.

At the start of the journey, the children expressed disappointment when they realized that their search for God would keep them close to home in Ewa. For weeks they had dreams of soaring through clouds in a helicopter, sailing on the open waters aboard a glass-bottom boat, or gliding above the ocean floor inside a submarine.

Soon, however, the mere act of seeking God opens their eyes to a world they had missed. The children learn they do not need to travel far to find God. They have been granted the singular grace

Lisa Maghamil, mother, age 33

Janeen Pasion, age 13

Shirley Castro, mother, age 54

BEAUTIFUL FACES, CURIOUS MINDS, OUR CHILDREN, OUR FUTURE.
WHERE THE CHILDREN ARE, GOD ISN'T FAR.

Lorra Naholowa'a, auntie, age 32

THIS PICTURE REMINDS ME OF GOD
IN THE WAY HE WORKS
SMOOTHLY AND WONDERFULLY,
BUT DESTRUCTIVELY.

Royce Guerra

Royce Guerra

of finding Him in their own backyards. In fact, they have the opportunity to witness the very heart of God. At the center of God's heart is love, and service is the greatest expression of that love. They see God's heart as they listen to the stories of the daring Coast Guard rescues and their willingness to risk, even sacrifice, their lives for others. They see God's heart in the Care Van ready to minister to the needy of Ewa Beach. They see God's heart in the stones lovingly arranged on the ground to mark the passing of a life. Debra Delizo, a grandmother, states simply, "God blesses us when we love and help one another."

Chapter 13

"I Find God in Imagination"

Kegan Tupuola, age 11

Aimee Lew, age 10

James Rickard, father, age 44

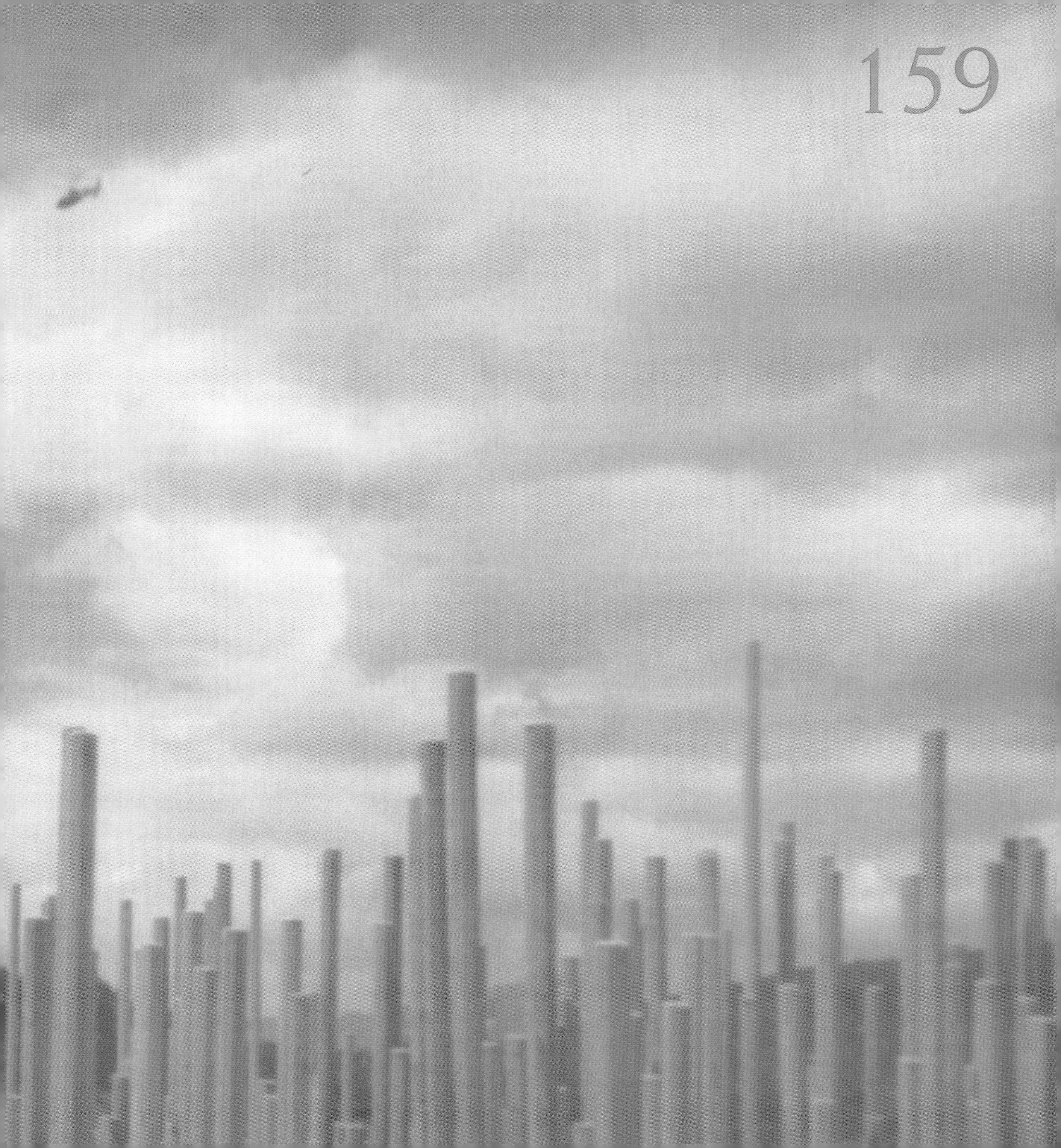
159

Jordan Tuscano

I FOUND GOD
IN THE WAVES
BECAUSE THE
WAVES ARE
LOVELY
LIKE GOD.

Holden Moi, age 10

GOD IS THE SUN.
HE'S THE BEST SHINER.

Jordan Tuscano, age 6

Seth Levy, age 9

I SEE GOD IN THIS PICTURE
BECAUSE ALL THESE PEOPLE
ARE LOOKING FOR HIM.   Travis Moi, age 13

Jim Rickard, father, age 44

THE CHILDREN BREAK OUT IN SONG AS BUS THIRTEEN ABANDONS THE EASTBOUND CARA-VAN AND HEADS WEST ON H-1. SOON EVERYONE IS SINGING POPULAR LOCAL SONGS, LIKE MOLOKAI SLIDE. BRENDA LEVY, THE KINDERGARTEN TEACHER, SINGS OUT SO THE ADULTS CAN FOLLOW THE VERSES. THE "SINGING BUS" IS HEADING FOR THE EERILY MAGNIFICENT WAIANAE COAST, A WORLD AWAY. They will beach hop all day from Farrington Highway, the single coast road connecting the local mostly Hawaiian communities with a series of great valleys reaching deeply back into the imposing Waianae Range on one side and the vast blue Pacific on the other. Local sunbathers know to come to these leeward shores if the skies are cloudy elsewhere. This side of the island is arid and hot, for by the time the moist trade winds have blown across the three-thousand-foot Koolau Range, the central plain, and the even higher Waianae Range, they have no more rain to give.

I SAW GOD IN WATER,
FLOWING ABOVE THE WATERS.

Holden Moi, age 10

Tammy Lew, mother, age 32

Tammy Lew,

I SEE GOD IN THE WAVES
BECAUSE HE IS THE WIND.

Emy Teis, age 6

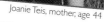

Joanie Teis, mother, age 44

TRAVIS MOI WAS SEEKING GOD.
I FOUND GOD IN HIS ABILITY
TO GO OUT AND FIND HIM.

Wendy Wilson, age 13

Joshua Levy, age 8

Nathan Conception, age 5

GOD LIKES
TO BE IN THE CAVE
BECAUSE IT SPLASHES THERE.

Jordan Tuscano, age 6

Jordan Tuscano

I SEE GOD
DEEP IN THE CAVE
BECAUSE IT IS DARK.

Holden Moi, age 10

The singers' first stop is Makaha Beach. Monster swells pummel the shore in winter and experienced local surfers flock here to challenge them. But in the placid summer months the ocean is easy. The children scramble from the bus and race through the golden sand down to the shorebreak to play tag with the waves. They lose. They'll be wet and sandy all day.

They go on to Kea'au Beach Park. Beach rock, visible and sunken reefs, and sharks pose hazards for any water enthusiast. But it's a lovely spot for those who seek solitude. Fishermen come here year-round.

I FIND
GOD IN
DREAMS.

Kegan Tupuola, age 11

Travis Moi, age 13

Jim Rickard, father, age 44

I FIND GOD IN MY SOUL.

Kegan Tupuola, age 11

THE BLOWHOLE IS GOD'S
APPEARANCE PLACE.

Holden Moi, age 10

Holden Moi

In summer the calm waves invite divers and snorkelers to explore the underwater world of the reefs.

The driver stops by the black mouth of Kaneana Cave. Legend holds that this 450-foot-deep lava cavern is the birthplace of the Hawaiian people and the home of Nanaue, son of the shark god. The children insist they must peer inside. But when they look into the gloomy darkness, they pull back fearfully and hurry to the safety of the bus.

Beyond is Makua Beach, with the dramatic Makua Valley as a backdrop. Hiking there is not

Travis Moi, age 13

Aimee Lew, age 10

MY HEART IS FREE WHEN I AM IN THIS PLACE
BECAUSE GOD IS HERE. I CAN SEE HIS FACE.

Tesha Malama, auntie, age 32

permitted because the valley was used as a bombing range during World War II, and there is still a danger of disturbing live ordnance. Our children enjoy the unexpected water show when waves crash on the shore and surge through crevices in the rocky reef. They are thrilled and delighted to discover dolphins playing in the waters beyond the outer reef. But another sight soon captivates their attention. An old truck driving the dunes gets stuck in the sand. The children want to run to the truck and push. The parents refuse to let them. Soon a white pickup appears and tows the stranded vehicle to the safety of the road.

The families continue on their journey in search of God to the last lonely sandy beach—Yokohama Beach. Farrington Highway ends here, and only the remains of the old shoreline railroad continue to wind Kaena Point. An eerie silence wraps around this group. They gaze in awe at the merciless crashing waves. Behind them looms the Waianae Ridge. Suddenly, the children spy a pod of whales. Their joy is unbounded. The smallest jump up and down in glee, pointing at the magnificent creatures.

Brenda Levy

ALONE ON A PIER HE SITS.
A FISHERMAN AT PEACE WITH THE SEA.

Brenda Levy, teacher, age 41

I SEE GOD IN THEM
BECAUSE THEY
LOVE EACH OTHER.

Holden Moi, age 10

Brenda Levy

The Singing Bus backtracks on Farrington Highway to Pokai Bay, the safest beach on the leeward coast. Our children enjoy their picnic here and wander by the shore. Then the families board the bus for their final destination, where irrigation has made the desert bloom in the form of the luxuriously manicured 640-acre Ko Olina Resort. They stroll the grassy park and the crescents of powdery white sand beaches behind the row of four shallow human-made lagoons by the Ihilani Resort and Spa.

The wild beauty of the leeward coast invites the God-seekers to dream. It is in this land of dreams that God and humans find each other and begin to shape the world. God is in each spark of creation—from the changing seasonal shoreline to the dark and deep volcanic cave to a half-built castle in the sand to the artificial lagoons of a resort to the naked steel framework for a new hotel wing to the bold and soaring architectural beauty of the Ihilani. God is present in all stages of creation. As one eleven-year-old boy rightly affirms, "I find God in imagination."

Chapter 14

"Finding God, I'm in Tears Again"

Mary Ellen Miller, teacher, age 47

Christian Nalumen, age 10

Nestor Ibarra

Nestor Ibarra, father, age 37

I SEE GOD IN THIS PICTURE
BECAUSE THE COLOR OF THE SILVER FISH REMINDS ME
OF THE HEAVENLY COLOR OF THE BEAUTIFUL KINGDOM OF GOD.

Hazel Ibarra, age 9

Myrna Ibarra, mother, age 37

GOD IS ONE OF THOSE FISHES BECAUSE THEY ARE ALL THE SAME, EXCEPT ONE. THAT ONE IS GOD.

Jennifer Ibarra, age 12

I FOUND GOD BECAUSE THERE IS SOMETHING SPECIAL ABOUT IT. THE EYES ARE LIKE GOD.

Jennifer Ibarra

PEOPLE IN THE YELLOW SUBMARINE SEEKING GOD IN THE GATHERING PLACE...UNDERWATER.

Mary Ellen Miller, teacher, age 47

Myrna Ibarra

BUS FOURTEEN, THE LAST NUMBERED BUS, IS THE FIRST TO LEAVE. THEY ARE ALREADY RUNNING LATE FOR AN AQUATIC JOURNEY OF A LIFETIME. ANXIETY MOUNTS AS THE BUS FIGHTS THE RUSH-HOUR TRAFFIC TOWN-BOUND ON H-1. FINALLY THE BUS ARRIVES AT KEWALO BASIN IN TIME FOR SEVEN PASSENGERS TO BOARD A CATAMARAN FOR A TEN-MINUTE RIDE OUT TO THE VOYAGER, A YELLOW SUBMARINE.

Four children, a mother, a father, and a teacher dive 120 feet deep in the Kewalo Basin. They explore a sunken ship

Mary Ellen Miller

Iris Nicole Saragena, age 6

Shane Duhon, age 26

Shane Duhon

Shane Duhon

Shane Duhon

I FOUND GOD IN COLORS. GOD PUT COLORS IN MY HEART-LOVE.

Joey Mecum, age 8

and the coral reefs sheltering this body of water. They stare at exotic marine creatures like the black tip tiger shark, sea turtles, and manta rays. Colorful Hawaiian reef fish glide past the portholes of the sub. The children are enchanted by the gracefulness of the bluespine unicorn and the sailfin tang. With only seven passengers aboard a vessel that typically transports forty-eight, this submarine feels particularly roomy. The captain and the crew are quiet so the children and the adults can focus on their job—finding God. But the children cannot contain their awe. Gasps and involuntary squeals of delight echo through the dim chamber. The children run from side to side to get a better view. Much too soon the submarine ascends to the surface, and the children emerge blinking in the sunlight.

Peggy Thomason, mother, age 36

Shelly Mecum, teacher, age 35

I FIND GOD WITH US
ON OUR BOAT RIDE.

Joseph Ubando, age 6

NOWHERE CAN ONE HEAR GOD
MORE CLEARLY THAN AT SEA,
IN A SAIL BOAT.

Bill Mecum, father, age 41

PRECIOUS
MOMENTS. I FIND
GOD IN A LOT
OF PLACES.
HE'S ANYWHERE.

Edison Vida, age 6

Edison Vida

THE PLANT
IS VERY GREEN,
AND GOD HELPS
THE PLANT
GROW.

Iris Nicole Saragena, age 6

Iris Nicole Saragena

Peggy Thomason, mother, age 36

Charles Thomason Jr, age 13

I FOUND GOD IN A STORE,
BECAUSE I BELIEVE HE SUPPORTS EVERY HARD WORKER.

Jennifer Ibarra, age 12

Cora Ubando, grandmother, age 55

The mood on the catamaran ride back to shore is quiet and reflective. They have visited another world without need of passport and ache to share this with the rest of their party left behind on the bus. Left behind but not to be disappointed. The driver continues with the remaining seventeen passengers on to the Ala Wai Boat Harbor, where they board a world-class sailing yacht—*The Free Spirit.* She's forty-eight feet long with a twenty-four-foot beam. She sleeps sixteen and is Coast Guard-certified to carry thirty-eight passengers. But today she carries only our families and God's crew. This thirty-one-year-old trimaran travels more than five thousand miles a year in Hawaiian waters. Her owner, Captain Gordie Morris, boasts, "This is the only boat that sails on the Word." Five years ago during a refit a Bible was encased in her new keel.

The children become sailors for a morning on the waters off Waikiki. They handle the rigging. They man the wheel of the yacht. They scramble to the bow and stare at the distant crescent of the Waikiki skyline anchored by Diamond Head, with the Koolau Range rising steeply behind. Some parents and grandparents are a bit unsettled by the motion of the boat and remain firmly seated for the journey, except when they feel compelled to reclaim their fearless children. The more seaworthy adults are as engaged as all the children.

The bus driver retrieves the submarine crew and returns with them just as *The Free Spirit* sails into the harbor. The families share a boisterous ride to Ala Moana Shopping Center nearby, excitedly swapping stories about their maritime exploits.

The children and their families continue their search for God in Hawaii's largest mall, which with its more than two hundred stores spans several city blocks. Our children are more interested in seeking God at the Disney and K. B. Toy Stores rather than at exclusive Armani and Neiman Marcus. Not surprisingly, they find God at the Cathedral Shop, a boutique dedicated to religious articles.

They spend more time in the central promenade sitting by the koi ponds and gardens and riding escalators up then down to Ala Moana's Center Stage, where shoppers are treated to daily island performances. Our weary parents and grandparents try to keep up as their children energetically pursue God through this crowded fifty-acre emporium.

Jennifer Ibarra, age 12

ALA MOANA PARK. THE PEACE OF GOD-PEOPLE RELAXING, FEEDING THE
BIRDS, PICKNICKING, SWIMMING, OR JUST ENJOYING THE SUN.

Mel Amion, age 67

Soon it is time to return to the bus for one final stop across the way at the Ala Moana Beach Park. The parents and grandparents are relieved to be able to sit beneath palm trees next to a lagoon and enjoy a peaceful lunch as the children gather at the water's edge to skip stones.

This day is filled with emotions for many hearts. Finding God is an overwhelming experience. Tears flow on the journey back to school as families share what this day meant to them. A father openly weeps as he tells his story.

Nestor Ibarra had not intended to come today. Many people were on vacation at his workplace, and he felt uncomfortable requesting the day off. He gently explained this to his daughters, Jennifer and Hazel. Their mother would not be joining them because she was sick with the flu. Nine-year-old Hazel, the youngest, decided to take matters into her own hands and phoned her father's boss from school during recess. She begged him to let her father have the day off. The boss summoned Nestor into his office.

"Do you know who just phoned me?"

"No, sir."

"Your daughter Hazel just called, and she begged me to let you have the day off tomorrow."

"She did? She is so desperate! I had no idea how important this is to her. I'm sorry, sir. I must have the day off tomorrow. Job or no job, I must choose my daughters." In the face of such devotion, Nestor was given the day off to be with his daughters. And Myrna, their mother, recovered in time to join her family for this day in search of God.

Our third-grade teacher, Mary Ellen Miller, captures the day with her open admission: "Finding God, I'm in tears again."

Bill Mecum, father, age 41

I FIND GOD IN THE ALA MOANA STAGE, BECAUSE HE GIVES A SHOW TO EVERYONE. GOD SHOWS US HOW TO LIVE AND LOVE ONE ANOTHER AS HE LOVES US.

Jennifer Ibarra, age 12

Chapter 15

GOD IS EVERYWHERE—AND THEN SOME

Justin Maghamil, age 9

Kegan Tupuola, age 11

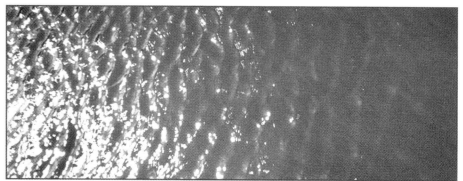

Jacob Butler, age 5

I SEE GOD IN THE WATER BECAUSE IT WAS FLOWING GENTLY
AND GOD IS GENTLE.

Keala Lee, age 12

HERE IS ONE LAST LOOK AT A DAY SPENT IN SEARCH OF GOD ON A LITTLE ISLAND IN THE PACIFIC. FAMILIES GATHERED TOGETHER, UNITED IN PURPOSE, RESOLVED IN FAITH TO FIND HIM. GOD DID NOT STAY HIDDEN FOR LONG.

Mother Teresa tells us simply:

I believe that God has created each soul, that that
      soul belongs to God, and that each soul has to find
      God in its own lifetime and enter into His life. That is
      what is important. All of us need to seek God and find Him.

This is a call to everyone on the planet. Seek God in your own gathering place. Seek God anywhere, and you will find Him everywhere.

A PATH OF LONELINESS
LEADS TO A ROAD OF HOPE.

John Mecum, age 10

In love, these captions and images gathered from all fourteen buses reaffirm that during one spring day God was indeed everywhere—and then some. God was found in the most surprising ways. He was seen in a lonely pitted path up an extinct volcano. God was found in a street sign, a chicken, a tourist's hat. A trash can calls a five-year-old girl to pause and snap a picture because, quite simply, "God made the trash can blue." Speeding along the highway, a seven-year-old boy finds God in the form of a truck because "that is His speed."

How can we all find God? A promise was made a long time ago.

Julia Cabinatan, age 15

David Moore, father, age 38

Christina Akins, age 22

I TOOK A PICTURE OF THE FLOWERS BECAUSE GOD IS PICKING FLOWERS TO MAKE A BEAUTIFUL LEI.

Kyle Akana, age 10

GOD MADE THE SIGN
SO PEOPLE WON'T GET HURT.

Ashley Wilhelm, age 5

"When you look for me, you will find me. Yes, when you seek me with all your heart, you will find me with you…" —Jeremiah 29:13–14

We gathered together and looked for God with all of our hearts, and we found Him.

Perhaps God is seen not through the eyes but rather through the eyes of the soul. The eyes can only perceive the world as it is, without God's presence—the material reality. To see God in our world, the soul's eyes must look for Him, because only the soul will recognize Him. The soul can see the divine

GOD MADE MAN BECAUSE HE LOVES STORIES.

Mel Amion, grandfather, age 67

Lorra Naholowa'a, auntie, age 32

I SEE GOD IN OLD PEOPLE BECAUSE GOD LIVES FOREVER AND EVER.

Joey Mecum, age 8

Pete Veglak, father, age 34

Wilton Wilhelm

I SEE GOD IN MY DAUGHTER BECAUSE SHE IS PERFECT.

Wilton Wilhelm, father, age 27

presence animating everything. By way of example, five-year-old Ashley Wilhelm found God in a blue trash can. Ashley perceived the divine presence behind our world. For a moment, she too lifted the veil of the ordinary to reveal the extraordinary swirling around us in every moment of our life.

One day on this earth a slice of humankind embarked on a search for God with all their hearts and found Him in their everyday lives. This is every soul's quest. From the moment we are born, we must seek God and find Him. Mel Amion, a grandfather, offers a prayer for the world: "I hope and pray that this day will make us realize that God and His love are still on this earth."

IS THIS THE SCHOOL THAT WROTE THE BOOK?

AS THE FOURTEEN RETURNING BUSES PULL IN ONE AFTER ANOTHER INTO THE TINY PARKING LOT, THE CHILDREN AND THEIR FAMILIES ARE DIRECTED TO HURRY TO THE CENTER OF THE GRASSY PLAYGROUND AND TAKE THEIR PLACE IN A HEART-SHAPED FORMATION.

The helicopter carrying the pastor, a science teacher, a mother, and a professional photographer is minutes away. This photographer will take one last photo for God's Photo Album, a group shot of all the hearts that found Him today. We hear the helicopter before we see it. As it comes closer, the crowd grows joyous until everyone—children and adults are jumping up and down, crying, hugging one another. We did it! A dream born in sorrow at the threatened closing of the school has been carried on the wings of prayer to this moment in time as a helicopter hovers hundreds of feet above. The photographer hangs precariously out the window, snapping photo after photo seeking the perfect shot. The helicopter lands in the

Thelma Parish, grandmother, age 73

vacant field behind the school and the "heart" dissolves and races to the fence to welcome the last of the God Seekers home.

The rest of the afternoon is spent breaking bread together at the gala, celebrating, singing, basking in the words of praise spoken by Hawaii's leaders, dancing—God lavishes His children with His love. Five hundred lives gathered together on our "field of dreams" relive the wonder of this day.

The Gala itself has been a miracle in the making. Evangeline Dionisio has gathered an army of helpers and has prepared a banquet to feed five hundred —in less than four days. The Gala Menu includes such dishes as lechon (roasted pork), chicken katsu, fried chicken, pork guisantes, fresh lumpia, hot-dogs, hamburgers, macaroni salad, rice, noodles, and fruit trays.

The dignitaries who have come to praise the achievement of this little school include Hawaii's former First Lady, Lynn Waihee, an aide to Governor Benjamin Cayetano, former Maui Mayor and candidate for Governor, Linda Lingle, Superintendent of Catholic Schools, Carmen Himenes, Associate Superintendent Louise Wong, and the principals from the Leeward Catholic Schools.

Mexican folkloric dancers, the school's choir and a local musician entertain the assembled company. Mary Ellen Miller and her husband Joseph serve as Master of Ceremonies. Print and television media wander through the crowd capturing this event to share with the wider community.

The Gala and this blessed moment ends in song. Shanita Akana, a mother from our school, invites everyone to join hands and form a circle. Grandmothers, grandfathers, teachers, mothers, fathers, children and the dignitaries reach out to hold each others hands while they sing a sacred traditional Hawaiian song—Hawaii Aloha—a prayer wishing everyone peace, love and harmony. Superintendent Carmen Himenes could not believe that this tiny struggling school was able to envision

and realize such an awesome day filled with miracles. Without God's help how could such a happening have been orchestrated? The gifts of 14 luxury motor coaches, helicopter, trimaran, train, trolley, submarine, and glass-bottom boat were simply astonishing. The donation by a generous community of three hundred cameras, developing costs, notebooks, pens and pencils fill the superintendent with awe.

In that heady moment we felt certain Our Lady of Perpetual Help School would be saved. How could anyone close down a school that was capable of this! News of the school's singular achievement spread throughout the island. And when the school submitted its request for a loan the following year, it was granted. Forty new students enrolled. The most common question heard during registration was, "Is this the school that wrote The Book?" Our Auntie Vangie would smile broadly and proudly reply, "Yes!" As the number of students grew, so did the school's financial security. The school's future was assured.

Weeks later, I joyfully called an executive with the Oprah Winfrey Show, and left an ecstatic voice mail. "We did it! Our children and families found God. We have four thousand photos of God and soon we'll have a book! Thank you for your prayers and encouragement. We love you."

Shelly Mecum, teacher

Hours later, Auntie Vangie rushed into my classroom with a message: "Shelly, run. I'll watch the children. You have a phone call from the Oprah Winfrey Show."

I ran. My heart was racing as I picked up the phone. "Hello, this is Shelly."

"Shelly we got your voice-mail today. Could you send us a galley of your book? We have never seen God. We want to know what God looks like."

I couldn't wait to share this news with production director Jane Hopkins and Bennett Hymer, the publisher of Honolulu's Mutual Publishing. A meeting was scheduled to discuss the future of the book. I ecstatically recounted *the phone call* from the Oprah Winfrey Show. To my amazement this exciting news was met with concern from the publisher.

"Congratulations Shelly. That's great news for the book, but it creates a huge problem for us! We can't go national. Our plans are for a local publishing. We are a local publisher."

My heart sank. "But the Oprah Show wants to see this. What do you mean you can't go national?"

"I'm sorry Shelly. You can either pull this book and seek a national publisher or let us publish it locally. It's your decision."

After much thought, prayer, and discussion the decision was made to pull the book and seek a national publisher. I closed my eyes and leaped off that cliff—in faith. What followed was a year that would test—to the marrow—this faith."

For one school year, I continued to teach and spend every waking moment outside of the classroom in search of an agent, publisher, and endorsements. During that year, I had absolutely nothing tangible to confirm that I had made the right decision, except for this flame that continued to burn in my heart. Whenever the light inside grew dim, God would send me a sign: a rainbow that would last three hours, a falling star that fell the moment I looked to the heavens asking God if I had made the right decision.

Thelma Parish, grandmother, age 73

Thelma Parish

And God sent angels. Wally Amos, author and humanitarian, was sent to me, I believe, to give me strength to pursue this dream to the very end, for my children and this community. He took every one of my calls and spoke only words filled with Faith. "Shelly, every 'No' brings you one step closer to that 'Yes'. And anyone who cannot see how extraordinary this project is—dismiss them. They lack vision."

Wally introduced me to his friend, David Allan Feller, who served as legal counsel for the project for two years—without pay. He became my personal guardian angel.

In the early winter, Mem Fox sent me an endorsement. This kept me wildly excited for months. She is an award winning picture book author and literacy champion and someone that I dearly idolize. I learned how to ignite the power in writing, the passion in reading, by studying Mem Fox's work Radical Reflections: *Passionate Opinions on Teaching, Learning, and Living.*

But the children's questions haunted me. They pierced my heart because they spoke straight to my own self-doubts. "Where's our book, Mrs. Mecum? What do you mean you pulled it? Why did you do this?"

I stopped everything to answer their questions. I was speaking to the children. I was speaking to myself. "Oh children, your writing deserves to be read by the world. You have no idea how powerful, how moving your photos and writings will be. You will change the world. Of this I am certain. But I have to find a powerful home for your work. I have to find a publisher that can bring our book into the homes of millions. To do this I need your help. Please, keep praying."

In the last week of the school year, God sent me another angel—my agent, Roger Jellinek. I met him at the Honolulu Writers Conference. I had also met John Loudon, my future editor at this conference. However, there was one more leap of faith required.

I learned that I would have to write this book. All along, I truly believed I could simply send 4000 photos of God and 300 journals to a publisher and they would put this book together. During a strategy meeting, I learned the truth. Eden-Lee Murray, my agent's partner and wife gently explained: "Shelly, what you have is documentation of an event. What you must create is a work of art. And you do this through the process of selection."

On the drive home from this meeting, my husband broke the silence.

"That's not what you wanted to hear, is it?" Bill gently inquired.

"No. It's not."

"Well it's really obvious. You are going to have to ask for a year's leave of absence from teaching and go after your dream."

"Bill, the school can't pay me. They can't afford to pay my salary and another teacher to take my place."

"I realize this. You'll have to ask for a year's leave of absence—without pay. You can't abandon this dream. I am more afraid of what will happen if you walk away."

And God took charge of the details leading to the writing and publishing of *God' Photo Album*. Believe me, when you seek God anywhere, you will find miracles everywhere!

At Christmas time, I flew first to San Francisco and then met with my agent in New York City. We had meetings scheduled with the largest publishers in the world. Another leap in faith. I was so afraid. But God never asks us to be fearless. He only asks us to be brave.

In San Francisco, I sat in a café on the Embarcadero, waiting for my first formal meeting with the publisher. When I got up to leave for the meeting, I clumsily knocked over a chair. I sat back down quickly in embarrassment and prayed: "God, I am so afraid." Then a thought wafted through my mind: "They're praying for you."

I looked at my watch and suddenly realized that my entire school, 200 children were praying at this very moment! And they were praying that I would find a loving home for our book. The fear utterly vanished and three hours later, I knew their prayers were answered. We found the loving home—Harper San Francisco, the inspirational division of Harper Collins.

My little school will be a beacon of Hope for the world. My little school will teach the world that dreams utterly come true—especially those that are powered by love, fueled with prayer, and driven by God. And dreams that are powered by love, fueled with prayer, and driven by God cannot fail.

During this spiritual journey I have learned two truths concerning the pursuit of dreams. First, when God asks you to leap off that cliff—in faith—You Must Leap! Don't look for the net. There is no net. I promise you, this the fastest way to learn to fly! Second, when you have leaped off that cliff—in faith; if for some reason your wings do not immediately materialize and you are crashing to the earth at an astonishing speed, remember this slice of wisdom from Wally Amos—"God always gives you a parachute."

Valleria Garcia

THE GOD SEEKERS

Ernie Aana, age 60, grandfather
Landon Aano, age 6
Patrick Aano, age 12
Deyandra Abella, age 5
Wade Abendanio, age 11
Alfred Ackenheil, age 5
Carlo Aguilar, age 5
Gino Aguilar, age 10
Jocelyn Aguilar, age 47, mother
Adrian Aguinaldo, age 7
Leslie Aguinaldo, age 13
Remedios Aguinaldo, age 40, mother
Sheryl Agustin, age 9
Andrew Agustin, age 6
Malory Ahlo, age 11
Shane Ahlo, age 29, father
Yvonne Ahlo, age 55, grandmother
Shaun Ahlo, age 6
Shane Ahlo, age 9
Lamborie Aiwohi, age 33, mother
Arthur Aiwohi V, age 6
Zachary Ajifu, age 9
Miles Ajifu, age 38, father
Bradley Akana, age 5
Brock Akana, age 7
Kyle Akana, age 10
John Akana, age 31, father
Shanita Akana, age 33, father
Jan Akins, age 44, mother
Christina Akins, age 22
Reisha Alcain, age 7
Rick Alcain, age 31, father
Irene Alcain, age 33, mother
Chase Algono, age 7
Antoinette Algono, age 29, mother
Jasper Alino, age 5
Stephanie Allen, age 14
Mel Amion, age 67, grandfather
Antonette Apeles, age 28, mother
Jacob Aplaca, age 6
Liz Aplaca, age 30, mother
Archimedes Austria, age 9
Helen Austria, age 38, mother
Irma Bajar, age 20, auntie
Genevieve Baker, age 6
Rachel Baker, mother
Melody Baldonado, age 7
Brian Baldovino, age 8
Carlo Barbasa, age 12
Nina Barbasa, age 45, mother
Jordan Barlan-Mattson, age 6
Donna Bell, age 9
Robert Bell, age 33, father
Lisa Bell, age 33, mother
Kimberly Ben, age 5
Bonnie Louis Ben, age 7

Judith Booth, age 52, teacher
Jacob Butler, age 6
Julia Cabinatan, age 15
Lourdes Cabinatan, age 52, mother
Remedios Cabrera, age 52, teacher
Buenaventurada Canubida, age 79,
grandmother
Nicole Caoile, age 13
Carlynn Caraang, age 13
Sherri-Ann Carganilla, age 8
Amelia Carganilla, age 33, mother
Cesar Carganilla, age 32, father
Paula V. Casamina, age 34, mother
Shirley Castro, age 54, mother
Virgie Chong, age 73, grandmother
Julia Chun, age 65, grandmother
Stephanie Closson, age 13
Daniel Colon, age 11
Johnette Colon, age 13
Jennifer Colon, age 30, mother
Juanita Colon, age 64, grandmother
Nathan Conception, age 5
Briana Conway, age 6
Evette Conway, age 29, mother
Maris Corpuz, age 9
Marco Corpuz, age 10
Leo Corpuz, age 12
Mirasol Corpuz, age 44, mother
Kenneth Corpuz, age 6
Joanne Corpuz, age 11
Judyline Corpuz, age 14
Julian Corpuz, age 46, father
Peggy Crowell, age 60, grandmother
Christopher Cruz, age 10
Genefred Cruz, age 9
Nicole Dacuycuy, age 6
Kimberly Dano, age 28, mother
Justin de Laura, age 11
Joshua de Laura, age 14
Allison de Laura, age 39, mother
Glenn de Laura, age 42, father
Jordan de Laura, age 8
Evan de Leon, age 11
Rodney DeGuzman, age 5
Jason DeGuzman, age 11
Debra Delizo, age 40, grandmother
Rose Delizo, age 10
Mark Deus, age 9
Ester Deus, age 35, mother
Davin Dionisio, age 13
Evangeline Dionisio, age 49
Joseph Domingo, age 5
Shane Duhon, age 26
Sarah Espiritu, age 8
Susan Espiritu, age 47, mother
Blaize Faurot, age 5

Michelle Felix, age 24
Jessica Fernandez, age 10
Tony Fonoti, age 60, grandfather
Aiona Fonoti, age 59, grandmother
Edgar Fuentes, age 6
Jennifer Fuentes, age 11
Fitzgerald Fuentes, age 13
Lucia Fuentes, age 39, mother
Gladys Gamiao, age 10
Philip Gapusan, age 7
Merebel Garcia, age 8
Russell Garcia, age 11
Mercedes Garcia, age 33, mother
Stacey Gascon, age 8
Peter Gascon, age 41, father
Ann Ginoza, age 13
Anita Ginoza, age 42, mother
Precious Gonzales, age 19
Royce Guerra, age 13
Rommel Halili, age 11
Beau Hannes, age 7
Jill Hannes, age 10
Kevin Hannes, age 36, father
Beth Hannes, age 37, mother
Heather Hauhio, age 5
Sarah Hauhio, age 6
Kellie Hauhio, age 27, mother
Jeannette Heringa, age 13
Julia Hernandez, age 6
Barbara Hernandez, age 13
Conchita Hernandez, age 34, mother
May Hilario, age 7
Rodrigo Hilario, age 10
Jovy Hilario, age 12
Bryan Hinkle, age 13
Bradley Ho, age 8
Bryson Ho, age 13
Cheryl Ho, age 34, mother
Araceli Hurley, age 28, teacher
Hazel Ibarra, age 9
Jennifer Ibarra, age 12
Myrna. Ibarra, age 37, mother
Nestor Ibarra, age 37, father
Christopher Jasper, age 6
Anne Jasper, age 32, mother
Denal Jenkins, age 13
Angelica Juanillo, age 9
Rolando Juanillo, age 50, father
Janinne Jurin, age 28, teacher
Isaiah Kaaihue, age 9
Zack Kaaihue, age 40, father
Justin Kessler, age 13
Ian Kim, age 13
Nani Kumia, age 62, grandmother
Lily Lambinicio, age 64, grandmother
Winifred Largo, age 56, grandmother

Keala Lee, age 12
George Lessary, age 11
Joshua Levy, age 8
Seth Levy, age 9
Brenda Levy, age 41, teacher
Aimee Lew, age 10
Tammy Lew, age 32, mother
Maggie Liuzzi, age 13
Trish Liuzzi, age 49, mother
Jarren Maghamil, age 6
Justin Maghamil, age 9
Lisa Maghamil, age 33, mother
Tesha Malama, age 32, auntie
Jovenard Mapanao, age 7
Joey Mapanao, age 38, father
Miles Mariano, age 7
Doria Maxey, age 12
Greg Maxey, age 39, father
Susan Maxey, age 35, mother
Loren Maybrier, age 6
Rosa Meadors, age 40, mother
Patricia Meadors, age 13
Du'Anne Meadows-Corley, age 13
Joey Mecum, age 8
John Mecum, age 10
Bill Mecum, age 41, father
Shelly Mecum, age 35, teacher
Mary Ellen Miller, age 47, mother
Holden Moi, age 10
Travis Moi, age 13
Priscila Molina, age 64, grandmother
Andrea Moore, age 9
Nancy Moore, age 37, mother
David Moore, age 38, father
Thomas Munson, age 11
Scott Munson, age 47, father
Sarah Myrum, age 7
Lorra Naholowa'a, age 32, auntie
Christian Nalumen, age 10
Evangeline Nartatez, age 5
Ignacio Nartatez, age 32, father
Joselyn Nartatez, age 28, mother
Rose Oasay, age 69, grandmother
Crystal O'Reilly, age 13
Mark Ornellas, age 36, father
Laurie Ornellas, age 32, mother
Janeen Pasion, age 13
Tiffany Peters, age 12
Elaine Peters, age 30, stepmother
Robert Phelps, age 57, pastor
Edona Queja, age 33, mother
Kylee Rabacal, age 7
Anne Rabacal, age 7
Minerva Rabacal, age 43, mother
Melissa Rabanal, age 12
Juanita Rabanal, age 38, mother

"I have called you by name." Isaiah 43.

Brandon Rafanan, age 5
Krystle Rafanan, age 13
Marites Rafanan, age 32, mother
Wayne Ramos, age 13
Denno Ramos, age 38, father
Rommel Raymundo, age 5
Rogelio Raymundo, age 32, father
Michael Recitis, age 6
Perla Recitis, age 38, mother
Earl Recitis, age 9
Tina Reyes, age 36, auntie
James Richard, age 13
Jim Richard, age 44, father
Jamie Sacayanan, age 7
Antonio Salizar, age 36, father
Maria Salizar, age 34. mother
Ingrid Angela Salizar, age 7
Sophie Sambueno, age 67, grandmother
Albert Sambueno, age 74, grandfather
Hattie Santos, age 72, grandmother
Kathleen Santos, age 9
Cecilia Santos, age 42, mother
Horacio Santos, age 48, father
Iris Nicole Saragena, age 6
Victoria Saragena, age 29, mother
Michael Sarmiento, age 9
Rochelle Sarmiento, age 33, mother
Bradley Sarvida, age 6
Leah Joy Sarvida, age 8
Myrna Sarvida, age 39, mother
Dennis Sasaki, age 54, principal
Jesus Schellhorn, age 6
Victoria Souza, age 8
Cheryl Souza, age 14
Anthony Souza, age 45, father
Gayle Souza, age 36, mother
Tavon Spiller, age 9
Linda Sullivan, age 40, mother
Gregory Suster, age 7
Robert Suster, age 7
Thomas Suster, age 44, father
Laverne Suster, age 38, teacher
Angela Suster, age 32, mother
Vincent Tabaquin, age 11
Bronson Taylor, age 6
Raquel Taylor, age 8
Pearl Taylor, age 60, grandmother
Michelle Taylor, age 32, mother
Emy Teis, age 6
Joanie Teis, age 44, mother
Coca Te'Moananui, age 12
Charles Thomason, age 13
Peggy Thomason, age 36, mother
Vivian Toro, age 70, grandmother
George Toro, age 77, grandfather
Leslyn Torres, age 12

Larma Torres, age 20
Karen Tracewell, age 12
Kaheanani Travis, age 8
Kegan Tupuola, age 11
Jordan Tuscano, age 6
Joseph Ubando, age 6
Cora Ubando, age 55, grandmother
Betty Uyematsu, age 75, grandmother
James Vahlsing, age 56, grandfather
Zachary Vahlsing, age 8
Pete Veglak, age 34, father
Edison Vida, age 6
Sharla Vida, age 29, mother
Kyle Villanueva, age 9
Elvin Ray Vitug, age 6
Adam Vorlicky, age 14
Ashley Wilhelm, age 5
Michael Wilhelm, age 7
Wilton Wilhelm, age 27, father
Matthew Wilson, age 12
Wendy Wilson, age 13
Lori Ann Wilson, age 37, mother

Wanda Adams
Mary Adamski
Marietta and John Adonis
Christopher Aguinaldo
Remedios Aguinaldo
Yvonne Ahlo
Air Survey Hawaii Inc
Patricia Aki
Ala Moana Shopping Center
Jack Alanza
John and Linda Aleskus
Dr. Elenita Alvarez
Sumiko Amakasu
Wally and Christine Amos
Alan Arakaki
Lance Arakawa
Francois and Lilian Argenti
Kris Ashley
Gabriel & Lois Audant
Augustine Foundation
John F. Baker
Nene Baldueza
Claudio and Rigolette Baraquio
Jeanne Marie Barnes
Sam Barry
Oscar Bautista

Tarre Beach
Wendy Bean
Harry Belafonte
Charles Bell
Sue Bender
Lisa Benoit
Tom Berg
Donna Lynn Bernadette
John Bibb
Suzanne Bile
Kristin Bowers
Bill Brazier
Mary Ellen and Jarv Britton
April Brown
Margery Buchanan
Rich Budnick
Pastor Kirbyjon Caldwell
Jack Canfield
Richard Carlson
Rosemary Carrano
Castle & Cooke Properties
Governor Benjamin Cayetano
Chasen Chess
Gail Ann Chew
Herman Chin
Sonia Choquette
Penny and Ken Christy
Charlotte Church
Diane Cirincione
Hillary Rodham Clinton
Cathy Chan Coehlo
Richard E. Cohn
Caroline Coleman
Mary Ester Correa
Bryce Courtenay
Ronald Cozo
Kelly Sue Crowley
Ferdinand Cruz
Margot Cueva
Sergio Curammeng
His Holiness the Dalai Lama
Fr. Michel Dalton
Regina Brown Daniels
Marleen Darras
Dr. Ajith and Manel de Silva
Teri Dela Cruz
Dr. Joanne Dempsey
Tomie dePaola
Brenda Diggs
Bishop DiLorenzo
Celine Dion
Lois Dippenaar
David Dominici
Mimi Donaldson
Patrick Downes
Philip and Manuela Dunn

Sue Eades
Jennifer Enderlin
Marian Escobido
Rep. Willie Espero
Rosemary Esquivel
Estate of James Campbell
Estate of Sumuel Mills Damon
Richard Paul Evans
Eloisa Evans
Ewa Beach Library
Ewa Beach POSTNET
Ewa Historical Preservation Society
Ewa Town Center Starbucks
Elizabeth Fall
Suzanne Falter-Barns
Kristin Fassler
David Allan Feller
Bishop Ferrari
Matthew Fitzsimmions
Paul and Michele Foco
Richard and Jeannette Foco
Illuminada Fortuno
Mem Fox
Free Spirit Sailing Associates INC
Roger Freet
Carie Freimuth
Fuji Photo Film Co. LTD
Ann Fujioka
Diane Fukeda
Sister Helen Gahres
Nelson Garcia
Valleria Susan LaRue Garcia
Dolores Gascon
Vicky Gaynor
Fr. Joseph Girzone
Mr. Globocnik
Kathi Goldmark
Tessie Gonzales
Fred Gonzales
Beryl Goo
Ishbel Mairi Gordon
David Goya
Kristina Gregory
Fr. Joseph Grimaldi
Ground Transport Inc
Steven Haia
Belinda Haley
Mary Hamus
Jim Hankey
Stephen Hanselman
Mark Victor Hansen
Mayor Jeremy Harris
Haseko Hawaii Inc
Hawaii Catholic Herald
Hawaii Literacy Inc
Hawaii Navy News

Hawaii State Library
Hawaii Visitors & Convention Bureau
Hawaiian Railway Society
Gerald Hayashi
Leslie A. Hayashi
Dr. Alice B. Hayes
Bob Hechtel
John Heckathorne
Cathy Hemming
John Hickman
Judy Hilario
Raymond Hill
Carmen Himenes
Mylene Hinkle
Lt. Governor Mazie Hirono
Don Ho
Elizabeth Hofstedt
Les Honda
Honolulu Advertiser
Honolulu Magazine
Honolulu Star Bulletin
Honolulu Writers Conference
Anthony Hooper
Hopaco Office Outlet
Jane Hopkins
Sam Horn
Karen Horowitz
Bennett Hymer
Darrell Iha
Senator Daniel Inouye
Glenn Ito
Troy Iwamoto
Diane Jackson
Hunter James
Dr. Gerald Jampolsky
Mary Lou Jardine
Roger Jellinek
Dr. Spencer Johnson
Alexandra Johnson
Anna Kainoa
Sister Norise Kaiser
Liane Kam
Kaneohe Bay Cruise
Senator Brian Kanno
Jeremy Katz
Dwayne Kaulia
Carol Kaulialamoa
Bil Keane
Kris Kelley
Patti Kelly
R. Kelly
Susan Ariel Rainbow Kennedy (SARK)
KGMB
KHON
Janice Kim
Tony Kim
KITV 4
Knights of Columbus Council 12045
Kristine
Dr. Helene Laperrousaz
Jared Matthew Law
Bob and Lynn Law
Leah
Sharon Lebell
Shoji and Jill Ledward

Janice Lehner
Madeleine L'Engle
Terri Leonard
Iregene Leong-Tabisola
John Lewis
Lewis and Lewis
Liguorian Magazine
Linda Lingle
Kehaulani Lobetos
Carolyn Kluckhuhn Long
Edward Lopez
Bob and Penny Lorence
Janet Lorimer
Los Amigos
John Loudon
Sunny Lucia
Libbyann Lui
Boe Lyman
Bishop Machebeuf High School
Cardinal Roger Mahony
Evan and Etsuko Maio
Makani Kai Helicopters LTD
Tesha Malama
Sharon Malloy
Nelson Mandela
Josh Marwell
Jane Marshall
Emogene K. Martin
Bill Matheson
Maui Writers Conference
Brenda McClain
Malachy McCourt
Frank McCourt
Barbara McElroy
Father Dan McNichols
Bill Mecum
Jack Mecum
Brian Melzack
St. Anthony Messenger
Kenneth Milik
Gary Miller
Dan Millman
Maggie Milne
Linda Mioshi
Missionary of Charities
Chris Mitts
Barb and Butch Moltane
April and Huey Monroe
Andy Montague
Jerri Moore
Nancy and David Moore
Tetsuto and Eri Mori
Captain Gordie Morris
Janet Morse
Rep. Mark Moses
Mother Teresa
Donald Murray
Eden-Lee Murray
Mylene Floral Wholesale
NBC News 8, Honolulu
Joe and Dorothy Nelson
Andriana Nolan
Dennis Oda
Minoru Ohnishi
George Okutsu

Judith Olenik
Nina Olmsted
Myra Pa
Dr. Wilfred Pacpaco
Sister Mary Bertha Paquin
Judy Parker
Alexander Paul
Kalani Pavao
Doug Peebles
Dave Pelzer
David Pendleton
Pat and Berk Pens
Eileen Pepiot
Rick Pepiot
Chandra Perera
Karen Peterson
Keith Pfeffer
Desiree Pilachowski
Mimi Pizzi
Pope John Paul II
Sister Edith Prendergast
Professional Photographers of Hawaii
Kevin Puahi
Leila Quinn
Jaime Raab
Veronica Randall
Chris Rauschenberg
Colleen Read
Read To Me International Foundation
Jim Redden
Hotel Rex, San Francisco
Pedro Reyes
Hewitt Reynolds
Dr. Jeanne Rigsby
Sister Mary Rinaldi
Robert's Hawaii Inc
Kim Roemer
Thomas Rollman
Brian Rosario
Jude Rossi
Denise Rowe
Roy's Restaurant
Rudy Ruettiger
Salesian Sisters
Charlotte Sasaki
Harry Saunders
Vivian Sawa
Richard Schuman
Helene "Sam" Shenkus
Betty Shimabukuro
Sig Shuster
Lori Silva
Sister Lorch
Sister Nirmala
Philip Dale Smith
Joe Smith
Ted Sodaria
Bob Solomon
Loretta Songer
Cliff Songer
Caroline Spencer
Stephen Spielberg
Janet Spurr
St. Anthony
St. James Elementary

Robin Stephens
Rhonda Stewart
Michael T. Stewart
Tonya Story
Anna Sumida
Samuel S. Svalina
Roque Tabiscola
Sharene Tam
Richard Tillotson
Brenda Timas
Dawn and Gene Tochihara
Dustin Tomonoh
Thelma Torres
Julie Torres
John Trifiletti
John and Shannon Tullius
Jan Tuomainen
Marlene Uesugi
University of San Diego
USS Paul Hamilton
Guy Vega
Lisa Venette
John Venette
Melanne Verveer
Alex Viares
Restituto Vitug
Domingo Vitug
Edelwina Vitug
Elenita Vitug
Patrick von Wiegant
Voyager Submarine
Lynne Waihee
Waikiki Trolley
Neale Donald Walsch
Jim Warner
Monique Washington
Gideon Weil
Fr. Allen Weinert
West Oahu Current
Adrian Whitaker
Captain Roger Whorton
Ken White
Marianne Williamson
Ray Wong
Gay Wong
Lucien Wong
Louise Wong
Gary Woods
Mapu Wright
Wyland Foundation
Elisa Yadao
Ron Yoda
David Youngstrom
Dwight Yoshimura
Steve Young